PISTOL SHOOTING SPORTS

A BEGINNER'S GUIDE TO PRACTICAL SHOOTING COMPETITION

KEN ADCOCK

COPYRIGHT

Copyright © 2021 by Ken Adcock

Pistol Shooting Sports - A Beginner's Guide to Practical Shooting Competition

All rights reserved. This book is protected under the copyright laws of the United States of America. Any reproduction or other unauthorized use of the material images or artwork herein is prohibited without the written, dated and signed permission of the author, except for the inclusion of brief quotations embodied in reviews and specific other non-commercial uses permitted by copyright law.

Publisher: Pistol Shooting Sports, LLC

https://pistolshootingsports.com

Email: inbox@pistolshootingsports.com

Print ISBN: 978-1-7350531-3-4

Warning: The information contained in this book does not replace hands-on certified firearm training and should not be used by anyone who has not received personal instruction in the proper use of a firearm.

The author, publisher, and copyright owner assume no responsibility for any harm that comes from the use or application of the information in this book. The reader should rely on personal instruction and training before handling any firearm. Firearms are deadly weapons, which can cause serious physical injury and death. Firearms must be handled responsibly, and the reader of this book acknowledges and accepts ALL risks associated with the use of firearms. This includes but is not limited to securing, transporting practice, competition shooting, live-fire, and dry-fire activities.

This book covers several aspects of pistol shooting, which is inherently dangerous. Never try anything represented or discussed in this book without full knowledge and acceptance of the risks and always follow the rules of safe gun handling on and off the range. It is your responsibility to ensure safe storage, safe operation, safe movement, and usage of a firearm at all times. The individual possessing and operating a firearm is solely responsible for the safe use of the firearm and is solely responsible for obeying all laws, rules and regulations with respect to the possession, use and transfer of the firearm.

Neither the publisher nor the author assumes any responsibility for the use or misuse of any information contained or referenced in this book. It is the reader's responsibility to know and comply with all local, state, and federal laws that apply, as well as how to possess and operate a firearm safely.

Disclaimer: This content and its products are not associated or affiliated in any way with the entities referenced within this book, i.e., International Practical Shooting Confederation (IPSC),

Steel Challenge Shooting Association (SCSA), and the United States Practical Shooting Association (USPSA). Furthermore, none of these entities have reviewed, authored, participated in the development of, or endorsed the information, products, and services offered within. All trademarks, logos, service marks, and domain names are the property of their respective owners.

ONLINE RESOURCES

Download the FREE resources that go together with this book - <u>Content Updated for 2024</u>

Dear Reader, thank you for investing in this book. As my gift to you, I would like to give you several **FREE** resources that will help accelerate your success in pistol shooting sports.

- Range Targets you can print and practice
- Steel Challenge instructional stage guides
- Dry-Fire guide with print and practice targets
- Technique Guides to improve key skills
- Links to key support resources for competition

Download Resources here:
https://pistolshootingsports.com/book-bonus

CONTENTS

Introduction   xi

PART I
FIREARM SAFETY

1. Rules and Responsibility   3
2. Storing and Securing   6
3. Get Training   8

PART II
OVERVIEW

4. Getting Started   13
5. Pistol Competitions   16
6. Divisions and Classifications   20

PART III
SHOOTING GEAR

7. Eye and Ear Protection   27
8. Hats and Footwear   34
9. Belts and Holsters   36
10. Magazines and Pouches   42
11. Equipment Placement   49
12. Range Bags and Cases   53
13. Trigger Action Types and Pistols   55
14. Ammunition and Pistol Calibers   59
15. Shot Timers and Journals   65
16. Practice Targets   69

PART IV
PISTOL SHOOTING FUNDAMENTALS

17. Overview and Training   73
18. Eye Dominance and Testing   77
19. Sights and Alignment   80
20. Grip and Trigger Control   91
21. Breathing, Stance, and Recoil Control   103
22. Draws and Reloading   110

23. Dry-Firing — 123
24. Measuring Time — 127
25. Malfunctions and Clearing — 133
26. Unsafe Conditions — 140

PART V
ON THE RANGE

27. Cold Range, Storage, and Carry — 145
28. Safety Areas — 149
29. 180 Rule and Safe Angles — 152
30. Finger off the Trigger and Sweeping — 155
31. Sportsmanship and Prohibited Substances — 157
32. Safety Violations and Disqualification — 159
33. Range Commands — 163

PART VI
SCSA COMPETITION
Steel Challenge Shooting Association

34. History and Game Overview — 173
35. Divisions and Categories — 177
36. Targets and Stages — 186
37. SC-101 Five to Go — 189
38. SC-102 Showdown — 191
39. SC-103 Smoke & Hope — 193
40. SC-104 Outer Limits — 195
41. SC-105 Accelerator — 198
42. SC-106 Pendulum — 200
43. SC-107 Speed Option — 202
44. SC-108 Roundabout — 204
45. Scoring and Classification — 206
46. Starting Positions and Strategy — 210
47. Training and Resources — 217

PART VII
USPSA COMPETITION
United States Practical Shooting Association

48. History and Game Overview — 223
49. Divisions and Categories — 229
50. Targets and Power Factor — 240
51. Course Types and Match Levels — 249

52. Written Stage Briefings and Diagrams	255
53. Chronographs and Ammo Testing	257
54. Target Scoring and Penalties	261
55. Stage Scoring and Rules	273
56. Stage Scoring Examples	282
57. Match Scoring	289
58. Makeup Shots	291
59. Classification System	301
60. Training Outline and Resources	304

PART VIII
YOUR FIRST MATCH

61. General Tips	311
62. Match Officials and Roles	313
63. What to Bring	315
64. What to Do	317
65. It's Your Turn	320

PART IX
MEMBERSHIPS

66. USPSA and SCSA	323
67. Clubs	325
68. Resources	326
Glossary	328
Acknowledgments	333

INTRODUCTION

Every time I see someone get introduced to the sport of pistol shooting, they experience a lot of pride and accomplishment just through their participation.

"That was amazing!"

"I didn't know I could do that!"

The sense of accomplishment and excitement is genuine—and *you* can experience the same thing. When I discovered organized competitive shooting, it changed how I viewed firearms. Shooting pistols went from being a target practice activity to a competitive sport I could enjoy with family and friends.

This book is the resource I wish I'd had access to when I started. It's written to help new competitive shooters learn quickly and experience success. The book and its companion website include guides and resources covering everything you need to get started.

The competencies learned in shooting sports are a great way to build knowledge, practice safe gun handling, and improve your technique. Not only will your skills and confidence improve, but you will have a lot of fun in the process.

Getting Started

For many people, an interest in shooting sports starts with a desire to do more with a firearm they already own or want to purchase. This book will help you understand how your existing firearm can be used in competition and what to look for if you are going to buy a new one. You will learn how to master the fundamentals of pistol marksmanship through the use of proper technique and learn how to measure your performance and skills. You will learn all about how to effectively compete in USPSA and SCSA Steel Challenge matches.

"I don't know what I don't know, so what do I need to know?"

This is a common sentiment when starting out. If you are somewhat new to the sport, follow the resources provided in this book, get training, get involved in a local club, and get out there and participate in the sport.

Being Safe

Being safe and having fun is what keeps people coming back to the sport. USPSA and SCSA organizations provide clear rules and governance that allow competitors to safely enjoy practical shooting sports.

Why This Book?

You will want this book if you are a firearms enthusiast or new gun owner looking to develop your skills as you experience the fun and excitement of organized shooting sports.

If you would like to save time, money and increase your abilities and confidence, this resource is for you. The pistol shooting sports are a great way to get out there and have some fun in the company of others as you advance your skills. *Get Started Now!*

PART I
FIREARM SAFETY

CHAPTER 1
RULES AND RESPONSIBILITY

RULES

The original four firearm safety rules were established by Jeff Cooper. (Jeff Cooper's Commentaries, Volume 6, No. 2, February 1998)

Firearms are inherently dangerous, so always be responsible and follow the rules of gun safety, including, but not limited to:

1. Treat all firearms as if they are loaded at all times.

Never assume a firearm is unloaded. Accidents happen when people assume a firearm is safe. Treat the firearm as if it has ammunition in the gun at all times. There is no exception to this rule. Respect the potential of what a firearm can do, and always behave in a safe manner. Always remove the magazine and do a safety check whenever you handle a firearm.

2. Never point a firearm at anything you are not willing to destroy.

Always keep firearms pointed in a safe direction. Don't point the gun at anything you don't want to shoot, and always be aware of where the muzzle is pointed. The muzzle of a gun is where the bullet exits the firearm when a cartridge is fired. In competition, safe directions are at the ground, at a berm inside the safety area, or downrange while under the command of a range officer. Always respect the fact that it is a firearm.

3. Keep your finger off the trigger until your sights are on the target.

Always keep your finger off the trigger and outside the trigger guard until you are ready to fire. This is important in any shooting sport, and you will be disqualified from the competition if you break this rule. Keep your trigger finger (index finger) on the frame of the firearm until you have your target in sight. The only time your finger should be on the trigger is when you are ready to fire.

4. Be sure of your target and what is beyond it.

Know what you are shooting at. Not only can you miss a target, but bullets can travel through targets and continue on. Always shoot within safe, designated areas and follow the range's safety rules.

RESPONSIBILITY

Always secure your firearms from unauthorized persons. Be sure you alone are in control of your firearm and have it secured at all times. It is your responsibility to prevent others from accessing your firearms.

Always keep your firearm unloaded until it is ready for use. Pistol shooting sports are *not* a survival activity, and all USPSA and SCSA competitions are held on "cold ranges." This means no loaded guns are allowed on the range until a competitor is under the supervision of a range official in a designated shooting area.

Safety First. The competitive shooter is always responsible for their actions, and this includes safe firearm handling at all times.

CHAPTER 2
STORING AND SECURING

You should *always* store your firearm *safely* and *securely*. All new firearms come with locks, and it is important for your safety and the safety of others that you understand how to secure your firearm.

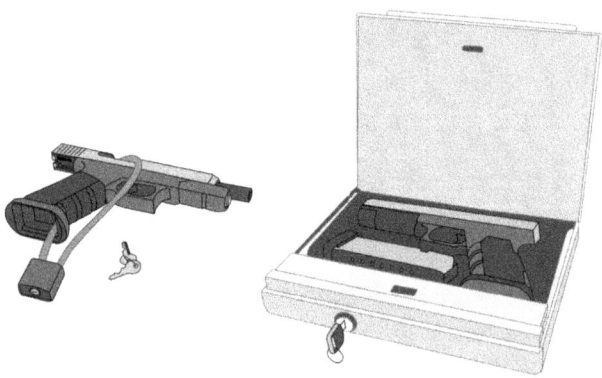

Your firearm should be locked and stored in a safe location and only used by someone trained and authorized. It is recommended that you store your ammunition in a different location from your firearm and keep your gun unloaded when in storage.

Safety Resources

Project Child Safe - Project Child Safe is one of the largest safety education programs in the United States. It was started by the National Shooting Sports Foundation and is committed to promoting firearms safety. See their website for more information: https://projectchildsafe.org.

NRA Gun Safety Rules - The National Rifle Association was started in 1871 and promotes safe usage and firearm education through many programs in the United States. See their website for more information: https://gunsafetyrules.nra.org.

National Shooting Sports Foundation - established in 1961 to promote, protect, and preserve hunting and shooting sports in the United States. The NSSF supports many safety and educational programs about firearms usage. See their website for more information: https://nssf.org/safety.

CHAPTER 3
GET TRAINING

This book and its resources are *not* a substitute for professional training.

Get hands-on training!

Professional training is the best way to ensure you have the knowledge and skills to safely use and operate a firearm. To find authorized instructors or classes on safety and operation, first ask the dealer you purchased your firearm from. You can also do a web search for certified instruction in your area.

Professional training will teach you how to operate your firearm and understand the mechanical attributes of your equipment. Be certain you know how all safety mechanisms work, how to load and unload your firearm, and how to safely recover from a malfunction. All guns behave differently in terms of trigger operation, resetting, and safety features. If you have questions about your firearm, ask your local dealer or go directly to the manufacturer.

For a list of local training resources in your area, do a web search for "certified firearms training" to see what is near you.

PART II
OVERVIEW

CHAPTER 4
GETTING STARTED

The best way to get started in pistol shooting sports is to attend a local match, observe how matches work, and meet the people involved in the sport. It's easy to find clubs using the USPSA and SCSA websites, as they contain a searchable list of clubs and matches that you can filter by ZIP Code or state. Each club has a registered location and contact information where you can learn more about events and how to participate. When you identify yourself as a new shooter, people will be happy to help you or point you in the right direction.

Rifle and gun clubs want to help you be successful. Every club will have members who will direct you to the people and resources you need to get started. Find those people, listen, and learn. Everyone started at the beginning at some point, so don't be afraid to ask questions, seek experienced advice, and educate yourself.

Observe how it's done: Start by attending a USPSA and SCSA competition. If you know someone who competes, have them take you to a match. You can also visit your local gun store and ask them where the local club meets in your area to see firsthand how a match works.

Talk to people: The shooting community, in general, is very open and friendly. If you identify yourself as a new shooter, you will be directed to people and resources to help get you started.

Things to do on your first trip to a competition: There are a few must-haves that include the right ear and eye protection, a good attitude, and a notepad to write down all the new information you will learn. If it's hot outside, I would also recommend bringing water, a hat, and sunscreen. Most ranges do not offer food, so a portable snack is also handy. To ensure your comfort, you should wear athletic shoes and dress in comfortable clothes. Most importantly, observe what others do before you participate in your first shooting competition.

People are there to compete and enjoy the sport, so introduce yourself and talk to other shooting competitors.

Safety: Safety comes first, and this is demonstrated throughout competitive shooting competitions. When you are on the range, all guns remain *unloaded* until it is the competitor's turn to shoot. Designated range officers will only give the command to *"load and make ready"* when the range is clear and the competitor is facing downrange.

Things to pay attention to: All range commands, rules, and safety areas. Consider the different kinds of pistols and equipment people use. Take note of the types of divisions people are competing in, how a stage is scored, and how competitors move and reload on a stage. Depending on the type of match you attend, it is beneficial to review the rules to become familiar with the concepts and topics you will see.

For an overview of rules, check out:

- Steel Challenge Shooting Association (SCSA) https://scsa.org
- United States Practical Shooting Association (USPSA) https://uspsa.org

Fees: Most range memberships and shooting clubs require a yearly fee to become a member. Match fees are outside of this cost. Most organizations have a website or Facebook page where you can view a calendar of events and learn how to apply for membership.

CHAPTER 5
PISTOL COMPETITIONS

There are many great pistol shooting sports where competitors can demonstrate their skills and learn how to achieve a new level of performance and competence. Below is a list of some of the most popular pistol shooting sports including an overview of the events and where you can go to learn more.

STEEL CHALLENGE SHOOTING ASSOCIATION

The Steel Challenge Shooting Association (or SCSA) started in 1981. Their focus is on speed shooting for pistol and pistol-caliber rifles. Events are held all over the United States, and you can find one near you at https://scsa.org.

The Annual Steel Challenge Championship is called the World Speed Shooting Championships (or WSSC). The winner receives the title of the 'World's Fastest Shooter,' and the SCSA maintains world records for each of the standard eight courses of fire. Recognized individual categories include Lady, Junior, Senior, Super Senior, Military, and Law Enforcement. Steel Challenge is a simple game of speed and consistency that all skill levels can start having fun with right away. To learn more about Steel Challenge, visit: https://scsa.org.

UNITED STATES PRACTICAL SHOOTING ASSOCIATION

The United States Practical Shooting Association (or USPSA) started in 1976. Their focus is practical shooting on the move for pistol and pistol-caliber rifles. Practical shooting allows competitors to strategize how they will use speed, power, and accuracy in competition. Events are held at local clubs all over the United States, and you can find one near you at https://uspsa.org.

The Annual USPSA Nationals competitions are divided into several large events by equipment divisions. These events span several days and test competitors' wide range of skills. Recognized individual categories include Lady, Junior, Senior, Super Senior, Military, and Law Enforcement. To learn more about USPSA, visit https://uspsa.org.

INTERNATIONAL DEFENSE PISTOL ASSOCIATION

The International Defense Pistol Association (or IDPA) started in 1996. Their focus is on sport-based defensive pistol techniques to solve simulated self-defense scenarios. Competitors use practical handguns and holsters suitable for self-defense. All pistols used in the competition start concealed. Events are held all over the United States, and you can find one near you at https://idpa.com.

INTERNATIONAL PRACTICAL SHOOTING CONFEDERATION

The International Practical Shooting Confederation (or IPSC) started in 1975. They have a number of major event locations around the world, including in Switzerland, Austria, Rhodesia, South Africa, the United States, Venezuela, England, Brazil, Philippines, Ecuador, Indonesia, Greece, France, and Thailand. A world event takes place every three years. Recognized individual categories include Overall Champion, Lady, Junior, Senior, Super Senior, and Teams based on country of residence. World rankings can be found at https://ipscrating.com. To learn more about IPSC, go to https://ipsc.org.

NATIONAL RIFLE ASSOCIATION BIANCHI CUP

The NRA Bianchi Cup was started in 1979 by former police officer and holster designer John Bianchi. The event originally began as a law enforcement training match. This event focuses on action pistols and is one of the most prestigious events in the pistol shooting sports community. It brings competitors from all over the world. Competitors engage once a year in four events over three days, where accuracy, speed, and precision are measured. The four events offered are Practical, Barricade, Falling Plate, and Moving Target. To learn more about the Bianchi Cup, visit https://competitions.nra.org.

INTERNATIONAL SHOOTING SPORTS FEDERATION

The International Shooting Sports Federation (or ISSF) started in 1907. The federation focuses on Olympic-style shooting using air rifles and pistols, and shotguns for trap and skeet competitions.

The ISSF cooperates with officials and committees that support the International Olympic Committee (IOC). Competitions include the ISSF World Shooting Championships, a World Cup, and a Junior World Cup. Other events are also held throughout the world across many supporting countries. To learn more about ISSF, visit https://issf-sports.org.

ONLINE RESOURCES

You can see a larger list of pistol shooting sports using the online resources at

https://pistolshootingsports.com/pistol-competitions.

Note: As you can see from the list above, there are a lot of different competitions to choose from. However, from here on in, this book will only focus on the pistol sports, semi-automatic handguns, and the shooting competitions offered by Steel Challenge Shooting Association (SCSA) and United States Practical Shooting Association (USPSA). They are collectively known as "practical shooting" sports.

CHAPTER 6
DIVISIONS AND CLASSIFICATIONS

In USPSA and SCSA competitions, divisions group competitors by equipment and require them to adhere to a consistent set of rules. Classifications define competitors' performance and skill level within a specific division.

DIVISIONS

There are five division groups in practical shooting competitions:

- **Customized High Performance**
- **Traditional Classic**
- **Stock**
- **Rifles Using Pistol Calibers**
- **Rimfire** (Steel Challenge only)

1. Customized High Performance

Open Division - These are race guns that are allowed the most modifications and high-performance options. Equipment is designed with speed in mind: high-capacity magazines, compensators, red dots mounted to the frame, and high-speed holsters. Most competitors reload custom ammo tuned for their gun.

Limited - This division allows for many customized modifications, including magazine wells, slide cuts, thumb rests, and frame and grip modifications. All limited guns must use iron sights only and no compensators. This division is very popular for iron sight shooters who want to shoot with high-capacity magazines.

Limited 10 - This division is similar to Limited but restricts each magazine to ten rounds under USPSA competition. This division is popular in states where there are limits on the number of rounds in a magazine.

2. Traditional Classic

Revolver - This involves the use of a classic-style wheel gun that uses a cylinder and hammer. This division uses iron sights, with a maximum of six or eight rounds, in USPSA competition. Advanced competitors use ammo holders called moon clips and speed loaders to facilitate fast loading and unloading from the cylinder.

Single Stack 1911 - This is for classic-style pistols that follow the original 1911 design by John Browning. Competitors use iron sights and may shoot a maximum of eight or ten rounds per magazine in USPSA competitions.

3. Stock

Production - This division uses iron sights (see USPSA Production List for models and weights). Factory guns compete against other factory guns, which is an inexpensive option and a viable place to get started in competitive shooting. Production allows for fewer modifications, so many new competitors start here, as they often already own something that qualifies. USPSA competitions have a fifteen-round limit per magazine in this division.

Carry Optics - This includes the use of Production guns with red dot sights (see the USPSA Production list for models). This division is popular for red dot shooters who want to compete with higher-capacity magazines.

4. Rifles Using Pistol Calibers

PCC - This division uses pistol-caliber carbines, which utilize high-capacity magazines, irons, and optics. These guns are highly custom and very fast. This is the newest division added to USPSA.

5. Rimfire

Rimfire Pistol and Rifle - .22-caliber, low-cost, off-the-shelf ammunition, fast shooting, and simple to operate. *Note: Rimfire pistols and rifles are used in Steel Challenge (SCSA) but not USPSA competitions.*

See this books chapters on SCSA and USPSA Competition for details on each Division.

CLASSIFICATIONS

Classifications define competitors' performance and skill. To become classified, you must have at least four scores in one division across four different classifiers. When you have shot more than four qualifiers, the classification system will use your best four (out of the most recent six qualifiers) to complete the calculation. Your percentage will reflect your classifier stage scores and overall match performance recorded as part of registered events.

Classification Scale

- **Grand Master** >= 95% (95 to 100%)
- **Master** >=85% (85 to 94.9%)
- **A** Class >=75% (75 to 84.9%)
- **B** Class >=60% (60 to 74.9%)
- **C** Class >=40% (40 to 59.9%)
- **D** Class >=0% (Below 40%)
- **U** Class = Unclassified

PART III
SHOOTING GEAR

CHAPTER 7
EYE AND EAR PROTECTION

EYE PROTECTION

Proper eye protection is a must for anyone participating in or observing shooting activity. Occasional small ricocheting fragments and hot bullet casings may fly your way, so you should use eye protection that fits well and reliably protects your eyes. Everyone on a live range is required to wear eye protection at all times.

Impact Ratings - This is one of the most important features to consider when you select eye protection. There are two prominent U.S. ratings. These include:

- **U.S. Civilian ANSI Standard "Z87.1":** Look for eyewear (lenses and frames), that have been impact tested to meet this standard.
- **U.S. Military MIL-PRF-31013:** This is U.S. military-standard eyewear which has been tested to meet the shooting standards for the U.S. military.

U.V. protection - U.V. or ultraviolet rays are emitted from the sun. Competitive shooters need sharp eyes and good vision for movement and target acquisition. Glasses with U.V. protection help maintain healthy eyes for continued performance.

There are two basic types of U.V. rays: UVA and UVB. The UVA rays penetrate more deeply into tissue and skin, whereas UVB rays are what cause sunburn and skin cancers. Both forms can be harmful to your eyes.

Look for eye protection that is rated to block 99% of U.V. rays. The safest designs are the types that wrap around your face, protecting your eyes from all sides. Selecting a darker lens can also help you see better under bright sun conditions, and polarization can add even more clarity.

Fit - As a competitor, you want to stay focused on competing. You don't want to be messing around with your glasses. Look for eyewear that offers soft rubber on the nose bridge and adjustable arms to ensure a custom fit. The weight of the eyewear is also an important consideration, as lighter eyewear will be more comfortable when worn for extended periods.

Prescription - If you need a prescription with your eye protection, check with your eye doctor or optometrist first. Let them know the prescription is for competitive shooting so they can help select the best option(s) for you.

EAR PROTECTION

Ear protection is critical. Shooting firearms creates a noise with a decibel level over 140 dB. Extended exposure to noise greater than 85 dB can cause pain and hearing loss. Anyone who is participating in or observing a shooting sport will need appropriate ear protection.

· · ·

Decibels (dB)

A decibel is a unit of measurement used to measure the intensity of sound or sound pressure levels. Our ears perceive a doubling of sound for every +3 dB measured. The diagram below illustrates the exponential effect of higher decibels.

(dB) NOISE LEVEL CHART

Level	dB	Example
Death	200 dB	
Severe	180 dB	Volcano Eruption
Pain	160 dB	Rocket Launch
Pain	150 dB	Dragsters, Shotguns
Pain	140 dB	Fireworks, Gunshots
Very Loud	130 dB	Car Racing, Jackhammer
Very Loud	120 dB	Sirens, Thunder
Very Loud	110 dB	Car horn, Leaf blower
Loud	100 dB	Pneumatic Drill, Helicopter
Loud	90 dB	Hair dryer, Lawn mower
Loud	80 dB	Vacuum Cleaner, Alarm clock
Moderate	70 dB	Road Traffic
Moderate	60 dB	Normal Talking
Moderate	50 dB	Refrigerator, Room Fan
Faint	40 dB	Computer fan, light rain
Faint	30 dB	Whisper
Faint	20 dB	Rustling Leaves, Clock Ticking
Faint	10 dB	Breathing
	0 dB	Total Silence

To put shooting sports into perspective: total silence = 0 dB, whisper = 30 dB, normal talking = 60 dB, hair dryer = 90 dB, car horn = 110 dB, sirens and thunder = 120 dB, fireworks and gunshots = 140 dB, and glass can shatter above 165 dB.

Any sound over 85 dB for an extended period can cause hearing loss. Exposure to 140 dB or more can cause immediate pain and damage to your ears, so appropriate ear protection is a necessary safety requirement at all times on the range.

Note: Exposure to 190 to 200 dB can kill you, as it causes your lungs to fail due to the increased air pressure and shock wave.

Protection Types

There are several types of ear protection to consider, including passive, in-ear, over-ear, and active in-ear, over-ear. The following describes the differences.

Passive - Passive ear protection is a plug or muff that reduces sound just by wearing them. Passive protection can be worn over the ear or inside the ear and provides a constant, unchanging amount of sound reduction. Both options are very effective and relatively inexpensive.

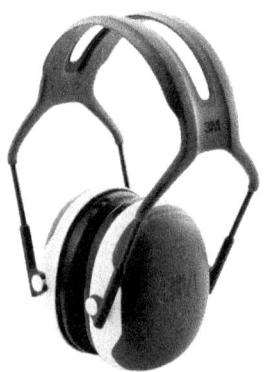

Passive Ear Protection

Over-the-Ear Muff - These earmuffs are simple to use and effectively reduce decibel levels. Different models have different reduction ratings.

In-the-Ear Plugs - These work well, depending on how they are inserted. For example:

- 50% insertion reduces 6 dB
- 75% insertion reduces 16 dB
- 100% insertion reduces 22 dB

Custom inserts - These inserts are superior to basic foam inserts, as they are molded to your ear's actual shape. Custom inserts are one of the most effective sound reduction options available.

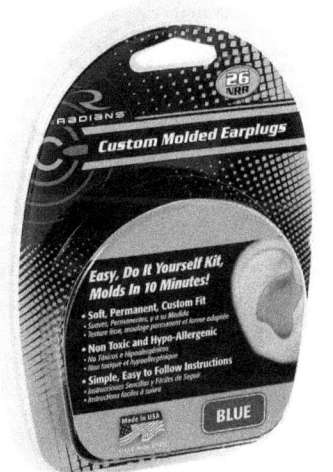

Custom Inserts

Active - Active ear protection uses electronic technology to monitor decibel levels and reduce sounds that are potentially harmful. They utilize microphones that only allow the user to hear sounds at normal or enhanced levels. When a sound is dangerously loud, the electronic device protects the ears by reducing the volume to the speaker until the sound level returns to a safe level.

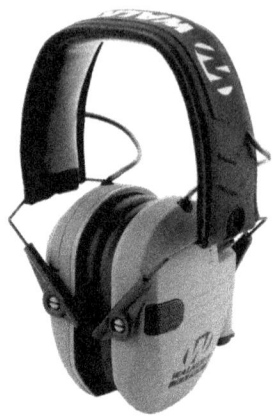

Active Ear Protection

Electronic suppression will increase your ability to hear voice commands but reduce the sound of a firearm that would damage your ears. Adjustable listening levels allow you to dial the volume to your preference. Some people combine in-ear and over-ear devices when shooting indoors, as it provides two layers of protection under very loud conditions.

SUMMARY

- Everyone observing or participating in a shooting sport needs proper eye and ear protection.
- Review and understand the impact ratings of eye protection before you buy to ensure the best protection. If you require prescription lenses, work with your eye doctor to select the best option(s) for you.

- Review and understand decibel levels so you can select the right ear protection that will protect you from exposure to dangerous levels.
- Select ear protection that allows you to effectively hear range commands during competition.

CHAPTER 8
HATS AND FOOTWEAR

HATS

It is a good idea to compete with a suitable hat. A hat helps keep the sun out of your eyes and allows you to focus on the targets without the light changing across your face or over your protective eyewear. When you are spending several hours in the sun concentrating on targets, you need something that helps your eyes stay rested.

Any hat can work as long as it fits comfortably, stays on your head as you move, shades your eyes from changes in light, and helps you focus on targets. Vented tops or backs help keep you cool, whereas adjustable hats allow you to establish the perfect fit. I prefer using a baseball cap with a curved bill, as it helps maintain the shade at the side and can easily accommodate earmuffs that help hold my hat in place.

FOOTWEAR

Most pistol competitions are done from positions where you are standing on your feet. Good footwear will support you and help you compete at your best.

Pistol shooting for Steel Challenge (SCSA) competitions does not require a lot of movement. Only one of the eight stages involves moving from one position to another on the clock.

However, USPSA requires a lot of movement, and you need to be able to start quickly and stop smoothly. Moving in and out of positions efficiently is how you save time moving through the course of fire. Furthermore, you may be required to move across several types of surfaces, from grass to dirt to gravel and even sand. Suitable footwear will help you stay safe and remain focused on targets and performance.

Experienced competitors wear sports footwear with large tread, which is effective on many different types of surfaces. Rugged, lightweight, trail-running, and hiking shoes are also popular. Choose something comfortable that will be suitable for use on the different surfaces you intend to compete on.

SUMMARY

- Select a hat that will stay in place as you move about a course of fire.
- Choose a hat that works with your selected ear protection.
- Hats that shade your eyes from changes in sun will help you stay focused on targets.
- Select footwear that allows you to move comfortably and provides traction across different types of surfaces.

CHAPTER 9
BELTS AND HOLSTERS

BELTS

Shooting belts attach at the waist using belt loops. They act as a stable platform to load out your gear.

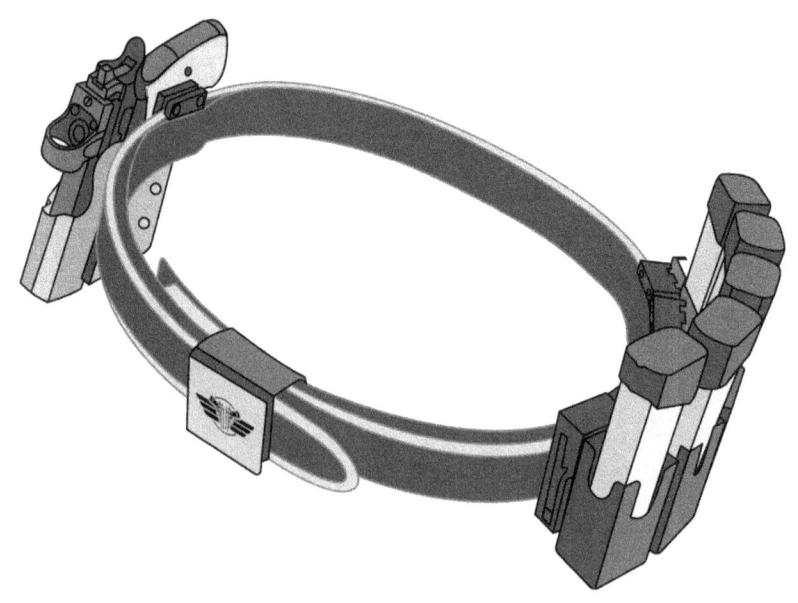

Dual Layer Belt

The belt should be rigid and support your holster and magazines so they can be accessed without moving on your waist. Female competitors may wear their belt and equipment at the hip level. When you add up the weight of a firearm and fully loaded magazines, it becomes heavy very quickly.

A one-and-a-half-inch belt that can hold the weight where you want it to stay will work the best. Competition belts are very rigid and are designed to support all your gear without sagging or changing position on your waist. Invest in a belt that will hold your equipment in position and help you build proficiency so you can stay focused on your performance.

There are two popular styles of belt designs: dual-layer and single-layer.

Dual-Layer

Dual-layer belts are made in two parts from sturdy nylon, which makes them very strong. The two parts consist of an inner belt and an outer belt.

The inner belt is what you wear around your waist and thread through the belt loops on your pants. It should fit comfortably around your waist and firmly against your body. The outer belt attaches securely to the inner belt using a hook and loop (Velcro) design. The outer belt is much thicker than the inner belt, as this is where your gear will be attached.

Both belts are fully adjustable using hook and loop designs. The dual-layer configuration helps to minimize any movement and keeps your holster, firearm, mag pouches, and magazines in the same place. This is beneficial because you want to avoid having to rebuild the placement of your gear each time you put on your belt to compete. The dual-layer design also supports a consistent setup that will help you master your draws and reloads.

Belt systems are available in many colors and sizes. Dual-layer belts tend to be more popular due to the lower cost. Plus, they fit standard one-and-a-half-inch belt loops.

Single-Layer

Single-layer belts are designed to be worn directly through belt loops and fit snugly at the waist. They tend to be slightly wider than a dual-layer system and can be made of leather or nylon materials. These belts are not as popular for use in competitions, as you need to thread the belt and attach your equipment using mounting systems. However, aside from this inconvenience, they work very well.

HOLSTERS

Holsters must securely retain your firearm, preventing access and activation of the trigger while your pistol is holstered. The SCSA and USPSA do not allow competitors to use shoulder holsters, leg holsters, or secondary firearms. When choosing a holster, make sure it is designed to fit your firearm. Holsters must facilitate a safe draw and re-holster, and they must hold the gun securely as you move about. Most models have ways to adjust the tension and fit to ensure safe and efficient retention.

Competition holsters must securely retain the gun at your waist with the muzzle pointed downward and the trigger guard covered, where the heel of the butt of the pistol rides above the top of the belt.

Holsters have two main parts: the hanger and the body. The hanger attaches securely to your belt, providing support for the body. The body attaches to the hanger, covers the trigger, and securely retains the firearm. You will want a hanger that consistently holds the holster body and firearm in the same position, as this will help you become more consistent with your draw.

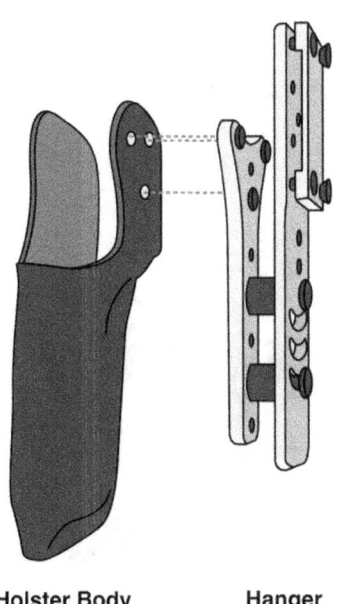

Holster Body   Hanger

The hanger attaches to your belt with the use of a mount that supports adjustable drop and offset. A dropped placement means the holster will sit lower than your belt, and an offset placement means it will sit a few inches from your body. Several mounts allow you to adjust the height or drop relative to your belt, and the offset can be customized using specific spacer sizes.

Types of Holsters

There are two primary types of outside-the-waistband competition style holsters: practical and race. Check the division you want to compete in, as different holster types and requirements are allowed for each division. All holsters must securely retain the firearm at your side, cover the trigger guard, and provide a consistent way to draw and re-holster.

• • •

Practical Holster

A practical holster covers the gun's trigger guard and muzzle. It has ways to adjust the tension and fit to ensure safe and efficient operation.

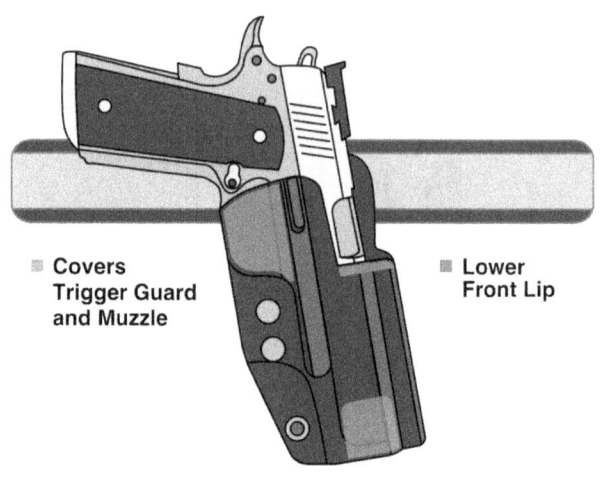

Practical Holster

Practical-style holsters are made from polycarbonate or kydex material and may have a lower front lip that helps you clear the holster body quicker on draws. The lower front lip should not be more than one-half inch below the pistol's ejection port when holstered.

Race-Type Holster

A race holster is very minimal and should be designed and adjusted individually for specific firearms. These holsters usually only cover just the trigger guard and use a special locking design to secure the gun when holstered.

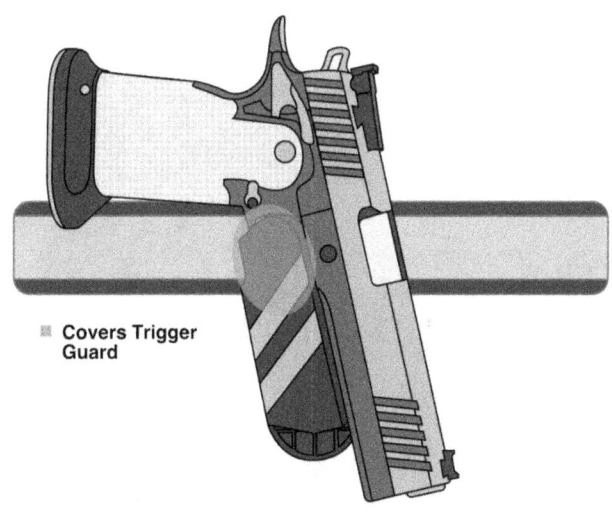

Race-Type Holster

The idea behind a race holster is that when it is unlocked in draw mode, you can present the firearm quicker. This is because you only need to clear the trigger guard compared to pulling the pistol entirely out of a practical-style holster.

SUMMARY

- Choose a good belt for your competition rig. Everything rides on your belt system.
- Dual-layer belts are popular, lower cost, and easier to configure by using the hook and loop designs.
- Knowing the pistol division you will compete in will help you select the best holster for your pistol.
- An adjustable holster's hanger will allow you to configure the best position for your pistol.
- A practical holster can be used in any division, provided the front lip is not more than one-half inch below the pistol's ejection port.

CHAPTER 10
MAGAZINES AND POUCHES

If you are serious about pistol shooting sports, you will need spare magazines. Having enough loaded magazines before you start a stage ensures you can reload and complete the course of fire efficiently. Steel Challenge (SCSA) competitions do not require you to carry your spare magazines, but USPSA does. Spare magazines should be located on the opposite side of your pistol and holster, as this allows you to quickly reload using your support hand.

SCSA

For an SCSA competition, you will need a minimum of twenty-five rounds for a five-string stage—and this is if you shoot it perfectly! A competitor with ten-round magazines could load five of them with ten rounds each to reduce any need to reload magazines during a single-stage run. If your magazines hold more than ten, you may consider bringing less than five magazines to get you smoothly through a stage.

• • •

USPSA

A USPSA competition offers the largest course of fire for a given stage. Therefore, you will need to carry enough ammunition so you can reload quickly on the move from your belt. USPSA stages are classified into three different sizes that correspond to the number of rounds needed to complete. Short stages are twelve rounds or less. Medium stages require twelve to twenty rounds. Long stages require twenty to thirty-two rounds. If your magazines hold ten rounds, you would need at least four to five magazines and magazine pouches to complete the largest stage.

You will want to have more ammunition on your belt than the minimum the stage calls for because longer stages pose greater difficulty and may require a number of makeup shots. To determine how many magazines you need, look at the largest stage in your match and do the math.

Example: If you have magazines that hold ten rounds, you will need at least four for a thirty-two round stage; whereas, if your magazines hold seventeen rounds, you will need at least two. After you figure out the minimum, you should add at least one additional magazine, as this will give you more flexibility when you reload instead of shooting the gun empty to a slide lock. The extra magazine can also be viewed as a backup in case of a malfunction, as you may need to eject the magazine to clear the firearm.

Magazine Types

Each pistol will use magazines that are designed to fit and reliably feed ammunition to your individual firearm. There are two basic types of magazines: single stack and double stack. The stack type refers to how the bullets are stored in the magazine before they feed into your pistol. Single-stack magazines stack each bullet one on top of the other. Double-stack magazines stagger the bullets into two stacks, which converge into one as they feed into the pistol.

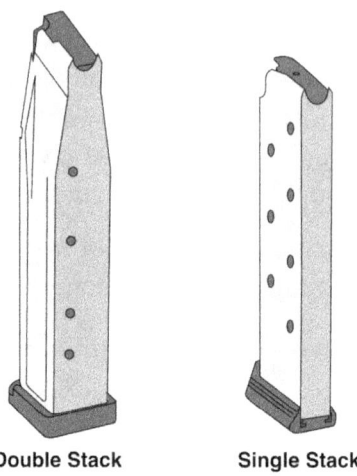

Double Stack   Single Stack

Magazine Types

Stock magazines are designed to feed ammo reliably into your firearm. Additional aftermarket parts such as springs, followers, and base pads can increase the capacity of your existing magazines. You should test the reliability of your magazines, especially if you upgrade any of the components. You may need to adjust springs and feed lips to ensure proper bullet feeding and operation.

Magazine Lengths

USPSA has specific requirements around magazine capacity and lengths for each division. If you are competing in USPSA, review the rules for your division to ensure you are within magazine length and capacity limits. Magazine lengths can be quickly measured using the official USPSA Mag Gauge. The gauge supports measuring both 140mm and 170mm length magazines and adds an additional 1.25mm to support differences in manufacturing tolerances (171.25mm for 170mm and 141.25mm for 140 mm).

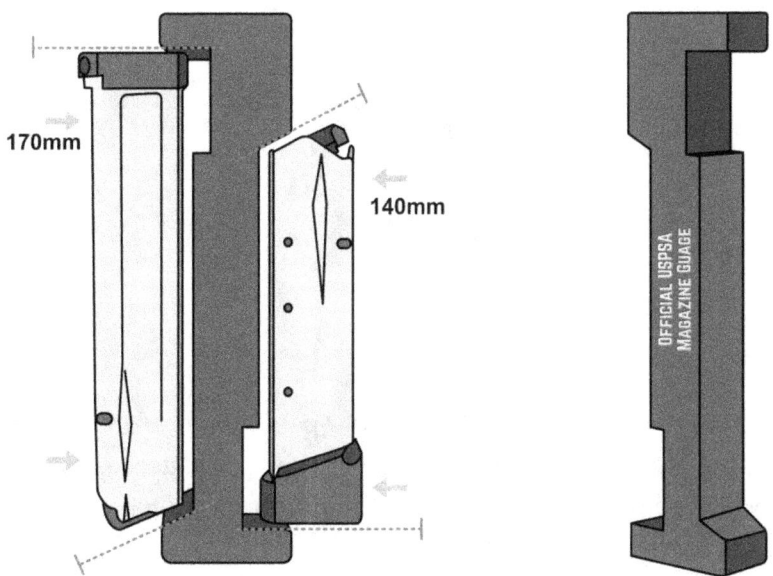

USPSA Magazine Guage

Speed Loaders

A speed loader is a tool that compresses the spring and follower inside the magazine so you can load bullets quicker. These tools help prevent wear and tear on your fingers, joints, and tendons when you are loading lots of magazines during a match. Loading several hundred rounds at a match will convince you that you want one.

Most pistols come with a basic, low-cost magazine-loading tool to help you compress the magazine spring and load bullets, but you may want to consider upgrading from the one that came with your firearm to something more advanced. Using a speed loader will help you load quickly so you can have more time for watching competitors and helping your squad reset stages faster.

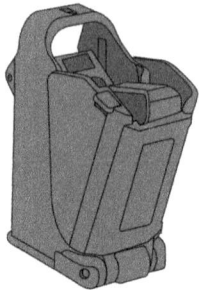

Magazine Loader

One of the most popular brands of speed loaders is called the Maglula UpLULA magazine loader. To use it, squeeze and pull down to compress the spring, then slide in a bullet. Releasing the grip sets you up to repeat the process.

MAGAZINE POUCHES

The most basic magazine pouches are worn on your belt and hold your magazines vertically. Pouches should provide the right tension to hold magazines securely as you move through a stage. Some racing pouches allow you to adjust the cant of the pouch to facilitate a more natural grip without rotating your wrist. When you can simplify the motions around reloading a new magazine from your belt, you increase your speed and efficiency, which, over time, improves your score.

Each pouch should securely hold a fully loaded magazine. There are two ways to configure magazine pouches: the bullets pointing forward, and the bullets pointing out or away from your belt. Aside from competition requirements, either method works well.

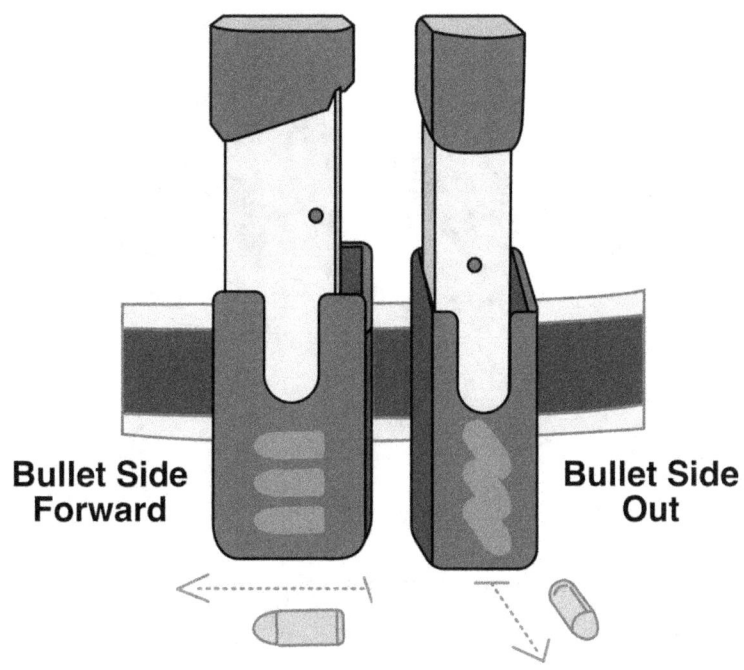

Magazine Pouches - Configuration Options

If you go with the "bullets out" option, more magazines can easily fit toward the front of your belt. This configuration is popular for competitors in the single stack division, where magazines that can only hold eight to ten rounds are required. However, if you are in a division that uses higher capacity magazines, the "bullet-side forward" option is more popular because it requires less wrist motion to reach back and grab a magazine.

Magnetic holders

These special holders attach to your belt and secure a single magazine via a strong magnet.

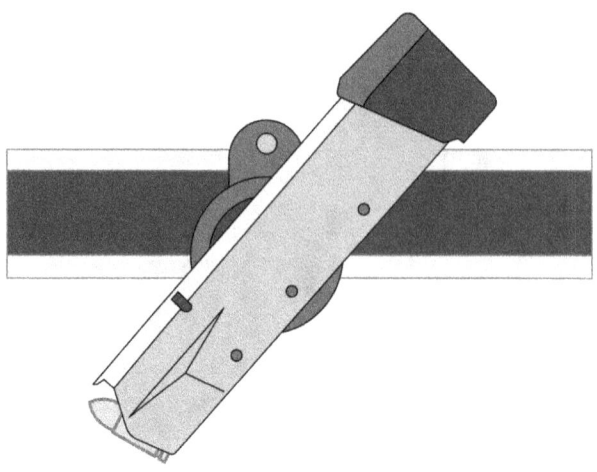

Magnetic holder

This design allows you to grab a magazine quickly instead of indexing one from a pouch.

SUMMARY

- Have enough of the right capacity spare magazines loaded before you begin any stage.
- USPSA competitions will have the largest courses of fire, and you will need to carry enough loaded magazines to effectively compete.
- Using a speed loader tool will save wear and tear on your fingers and joints as you load magazines.
- Magazine pouches can be configured two ways: bullets forward for faster indexing, or bullets out when you need to carry more lower capacity magazines.
- Magnetic holders are a fast way to secure and access magazines from your belt.

CHAPTER 11
EQUIPMENT PLACEMENT

It is beneficial to understand the rules for the division you have chosen so you can select the right equipment to be competitive in that division.

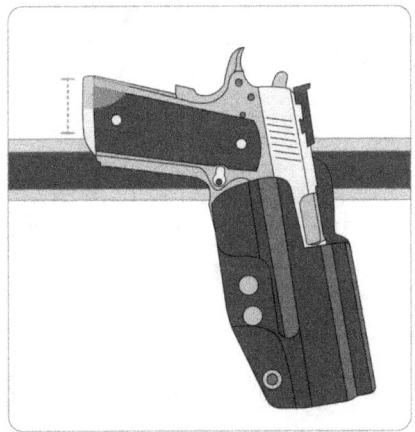

Holstered height

Holstered height

All pistols have a holstered height requirement that specifies the heel of the butt of the gun must not drop below the top of the belt when holstered. *Note: The holstered height measurement excludes pistol magazine wells.*

Lateral Distance Requirement

The lateral distance requirement specifies the maximum distance for pistols and magazines when retained by a holster or magazine pouch. The measurement is different depending on the division and is measured from the inner side of the belt to the equipment.

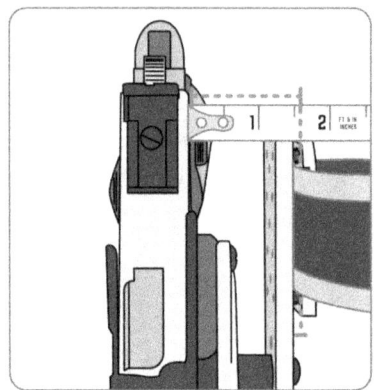 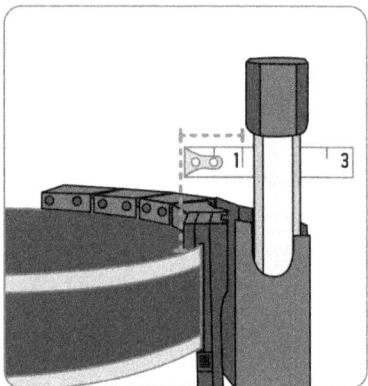

Lateral Distance

Specific division requirements for holster type and maximum lateral distances are covered in the next section.

Limited and Open Divisions

Limited and Open divisions give you the most equipment choices. The maximum lateral distance for Limited and Open divisions is three and three-eighth inches. Competitors may use any practical- or race-type holster positioned on the belt that complies with USPSA and SCSA rules.

• • •

Single Stack 1911 Division

The Single Stack 1911 division requires a practical-style holster and magazines. The maximum lateral distance for the Single Stack 1911 division is two and one-eighth inches. Competitors may use any practical holster that complies with USPSA and SCSA rules. No race holsters are permitted.

Production and Carry Optics Divisions

The Production and Carry Optics divisions require a practical-style holster that complies with USPSA and SCSA rules. Race holsters are not permitted. The maximum lateral distance for a pistol and magazine is two and one-eighth inches.

Revolver Division

The Revolver division has a maximum lateral distance of two and one-eighth inches. Competitors may use any practical- or race-style holster that complies with USPSA and SCSA rules. Revolvers don't have ejection ports, so you only need to ensure the trigger guard is covered and the revolver is securely held in place.

Testing

You can test different placements and angles by practicing your draws and reloads in dry-fire, without any ammunition present. When you move your hands to your sides, sense the best location to position your equipment. Try holding your hands above your head and then moving them down to your sides. Your wrists and hands naturally rest in consistent locations. Practice with different placements of the holster until you settle on the one that comes naturally. Proper placement will allow you to have a more consistent draw and reload execution. Always measure your equipment configuration to ensure it is compliant with division rules.

SUMMARY

- Equipment lateral distance is dependent on the division you will compete in. Review the rules for the division you want to compete in before you invest in equipment and upgrades.
- All pistols have a holstered height requirement that specifies the heel of the butt of the gun must not drop below the top of the belt when holstered.
- Test your equipment placement by practicing draws and reloads in dry-fire, without ammunition present, to find the configuration that works best for you.

CHAPTER 12
RANGE BAGS AND CASES

Every competitive pistol shooter needs a range bag or backpack to carry their pistol, magazines, and ammunition. You don't need anything fancy when starting out. Many people use an existing soft-sided bag they have around the house.

Range bags come in all shapes and sizes, and as you attend different events, you will see competitors with dedicated equipment bags and backpacks designed for competitive shooting. Ask other people what they like about their bags so you can start to form your own ideas of what you will require.

Specialized Gear Bags

A specialized gear bag is designed to carry pistols, magazines, ammunition, hearing protection, eye protection, speed loaders, timers, extra batteries, a bag to pick up spent brass, tools, a rag, Band-Aids, sunscreen, and other additional parts. The bag will be organized in an efficient way so equipment can be found quickly.

Having a bag where you can locate what you need all in one place makes going to the range a lot easier and a lot more enjoyable. It also helps you to focus on your performance. When competing, you will be able to move from stage to stage confidently knowing your bag can support you with everything necessary.

What to Look for When Choosing a Bag:

Keep an eye out for well-constructed bags with enough space to accommodate all your match gear. You will want a pistol sleeve or zipper bag to safely transport your firearm to the safety area before you place it in your holster. Look for bags that have specialized compartments where you can store your hearing and eye protection. It is nice to have a flexible area to store ammo, a place for tools, and an area for personal items. Be sure to select something that has a strap that can be slung over your shoulder, as this will help free up your hands when you are transporting your gear.

SUMMARY

- Every competitor needs something to carry their equipment and ammunition in when on the range.
- Range bags come in all shapes and sizes, so check out what others are using as you shop for the features that matter to you.
- Separate storage compartments can help you organize your equipment and access it when you need it.
- A pistol sleeve or zippered bag is very helpful to transport just your pistol to and from the safety area.

CHAPTER 13
TRIGGER ACTION TYPES AND PISTOLS

TRIGGER ACTION TYPES

Trigger actions refer to how a firearm operates with each trigger press. There are two basic types of trigger actions: single-action and double-action. Some firearms incorporate both.

The trigger action releases the striker or hammer, so it causes the primer on a cartridge to be struck and fire a shot. Depending on the action type, other operations (to prepare the firearm to fire) may be tied to each trigger press.

A striker-fired gun uses a striker rod or firing pin driven by a spring that hits the bullet primer. Striker-fired handguns are very popular and straightforward to operate. These designs incorporate the safety mechanism into the trigger, and all the firing mechanisms are internal to the firearm.

A hammer-fired design uses a hinged lever that strikes a firing pin that hits the bullet primer. Hammer-fired designs are used in 1911 designs, revolvers, and many competition pistols.

• • •

Single-Action (SA)

The single-action trigger performs one action for each trigger pull. That signal action releases the striker or hammer, so it hits the bullet primer and the gun fires. Because single-action is just a simple release operation, it takes another action (recoiling of the slide on the pistol) to cock the hammer/striker for the next shot. The single action is usually a lighter trigger pull, because it is only performing one action to fire the pistol.

Double-Action (DA)/Double-Action Only (DAO)

The double-action trigger performs two actions for each trigger pull. Each trigger press will cock the hammer or firing pin, then release them. Revolvers provide a good example of a double-action-only design because you can see both actions at work as you pull the trigger. When you start to pull the trigger, the cylinder will rotate by moving the cartridge into place. Then the hammer is pulled back in preparation to fire. As you continue through the press, the cylinder stops, and the hammer is released. A double-action trigger can feel heavier, as it is performing two operations in order to fire the pistol.

Double-Action/Single-Action (DA/SA)

Double-action and single-action pistols start in double-action for the first trigger pull, then they perform in single-action thereafter. This means the first trigger press will cock the hammer or striker and fire a shot. The recoil from the first shot will cause the pistol to cycle. The cycling is used to load another cartridge and cock the hammer or striker. The subsequent trigger pulls will be single action, because the cycling with each recoil is used to prep the pistol for the next shot.

PISTOLS

One of the most important decisions when starting is what pistol you will be shooting. An existing handgun that you already own is a great place to start—and using it in a shooting sport will help you become even more proficient.

If you don't own a gun suitable for competition, ask a friend or somebody you know who is already in the sport to help you select the right firearm. Making the right selection the first time will save you time and money later on. Understanding the different competitive divisions will help you know what features are important.

Avoid investing a lot of money on equipment when you start. It is beneficial to build on your experience in the sport first. When attending matches, observe what other competitors use and ask them about their gear. By doing a little homework before you buy, you will save money and time investing in only what you need.

If you need to purchase a new firearm, buy quality, name-brand items from established dealers that will assist you when you have questions or need help. Firearms and quality equipment, when maintained, will last generations. You don't need to have the newest, top-of-the-line, expensive firearm to begin competitive shooting. You can get started in Steel Challenge (SCSA) competitions with something as simple as a .22 pistol. For USPSA matches, you will need at least a 9mm pistol. Do your homework on what calibers are allowed in the sport you want to compete in and consider what works best for you. Most new competitors go with a name-brand pistol that allows them to focus on learning the sport and how to compete safely.

When you are starting, it is much easier to use a striker-fired or trigger-safety type of pistol. The advantage of this is that the safety is in the trigger, so it's one less thing to manage. For example, each pull of the trigger releases the safety and fires a single shot. Since the trigger pull is consistent for each shot, you can easily stay focused on your technique.

SUMMARY

- Don't spend money on gear until you know what you need.
- Seek out other competitors' advice and experience when getting started.
- Understand the different trigger types and ask your gun dealer to show you examples of each type.
- Buy quality name brands from established dealers that will help you when you have questions.
- Understand the division requirements for the sports you want to compete in before you buy.

CHAPTER 14
AMMUNITION AND PISTOL CALIBERS

AMMUNITION

You will know, when entering a competition, what the needed round count is to shoot a perfect match. Most competitions are less than 250 rounds. Therefore, it is a good idea to keep 400 rounds in your bag. This enables you to take extra shots or reshoot a stage due to target or equipment failures. Always check the round count of a match before you attend so you come prepared with enough ammunition.

Most off-the-shelf ammunition is good enough to get you started, but you want to ensure that you get ammunition that is designed to work with your gun. Check the specifications on your pistol and ammunition to ensure you have the correct match, as the pistol should cycle and perform as designed. See the original manufacturer's manual that came with your pistol to ensure you are selecting and using the correct ammunition.

It is recommended that you try several bullet weights from a number of manufacturers to determine what suits you and your pistol. You may notice a higher recoil with different bullet weights and different timing as the gun cycles. Try a box of ammunition using the same bullet weight across different manufacturers to find the right fit for you and your gun.

Note: After you find the ammo you like, try to use it consistently. You should notice that different grain bullets (for example, 9mm 115 GR, 124 GR, and 147 GR) may all work, but will change the timing and felt recoil. When you shoot the same cartridge type, and bullet size, it will help your consistency.

Popular Pistol Bullet Types

Below are three popular pistol bullet types. (Round Nose, Hollow Point, Flat Point) Round Nose bullets were designed to feed smoothly for semi-auto firearms. Hollow Points were designed to expand on impact and Flat Points were designed to create more force on impact. All three work well in competition.

Round Nose   Hollow Point   Flat Point

Caliber vs. Weight

Caliber is the measure of a bullet's overall diameter. Caliber can be measured in millimeters or inches; whereas a bullet's weight is measured in grains—the larger the number, the heavier the bullet.

PISTOL CALIBERS

Below is a list and description of the most popular calibers used in pistol shooting sports.

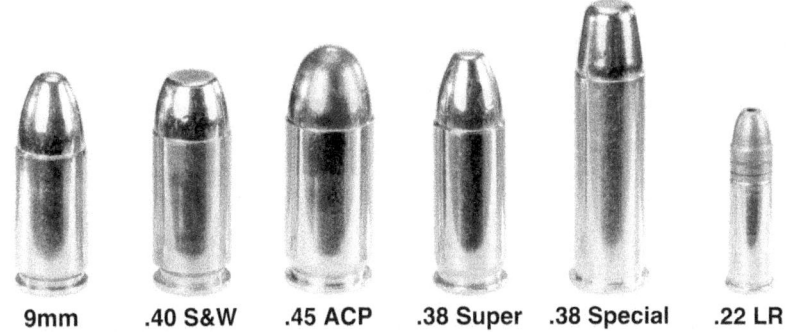

9mm   .40 S&W   .45 ACP   .38 Super   .38 Special   .22 LR

9mm Luger

Introduced in 1902, the 9mm Luger is the most widely used handgun cartridge around the world. It was designed by Georg Luger, a German firearm designer, and is used by law enforcement, military, and NATO forces.

The 9mm cartridge goes by several names: the 9mm Luger, 9mm Parabellum, and the 9x19 Parabellum. Rounds are relatively low cost, have low recoil, and have a flat trajectory. The cartridge incorporates a tapered case wall and was designed for small pistol primers. Common bullet weights in grains include 115, 124, 135, and 147.

Common Caliber names: 9mm, 9mm Luger, 9mm NATO, 9x19mm, 9mm Parabellum.

.40 Smith & Wesson (S&W)

The .40 Smith & Wesson was introduced in 1990 at the FBI's request. It was designed by Bob Klunk and developed by American firearms manufacturers, Winchester and Smith & Wesson.

It was originally designed for law enforcement to compete with the 10mm Auto, but the smaller design of the .40 S&W allowed it to work in similar 9mm frame designs. The round has more energy than a 9mm, and less recoil than a 10mm Auto. The cartridge incorporates a straight case wall and was designed to use small pistol primers. Common bullet weights in grains include 135, 155, 165, 180, and 200.

Common Caliber names: .40 S&W, .40 caliber, 10x22mm.

.45 ACP

This cartridge was introduced in 1905 as part of the prototype Colt semi-automatic pistol (aka 1911).

It was designed by John Moses Browning, an American firearms designer, and has been used by the U.S. military, the U.S. cavalry, police, and single-stack, large-caliber sport shooters. The cartridge incorporates a straight case wall and was designed to use a large pistol primer. (Note: Some Production ammunition versions are designed to work with small pistol primers.) Common bullet weights in grains include 185, 200, and 230.

Common Caliber names: .45, .45 ACP, .45 Auto, .45 Colt.

.38 Super

The .38 Super was introduced in 1929. It was designed by John Moses Browning, an American firearms designer, and emerged from development around the same time as the .38 ACP (automatic) and Colt M1900 pistol.

The cartridge was used by U.S. law enforcement and in Latin America, where there was a restriction on 9mm and .45 ACP. It made a comeback in competitive shooting due to its ability to hit a major power factor with low recoil. Rounds have good accuracy, high muzzle velocity, and a flat trajectory. The cartridge incorporates a straight case wall and was designed to use small pistol primers. Common bullet weights in grains include 115, 124, 125, 129, 130, and 147.

Common Caliber names: .38 Super, .38 Super +P, .38 Super Auto, .38 Super ACP, .38 Colt Super Automatic, .38 caliber.

.357 Magnum/.38 Special

The .38 Special was introduced in 1898 for law enforcement and military activities and is known as one of the most popular revolver cartridges ever made because of its accuracy and mild recoil. It was originally developed by Smith & Wesson and is designed for lead bullets and subsonic loads.

The .357 Magnum was introduced in 1934 as a higher-pressure cartridge with greater stopping power. Many refer to this as the second generation of the .38 Special.

The .357 uses a longer cartridge than the .38 Special, so pistols chambered in .38 Special only don't support shooting the longer .357 Magnum cartridges.

The cartridge incorporates a straight case wall and was designed to use small pistol and small pistol Magnum primers. Common bullet weights in grains include 100, 110, 125, 130, 145, 148, and 158.

Common Caliber names: .357 Mag, .357 S&W Magnum, .38 Special.

.22 Long Rifle/Rimfire

The .22 long rifle cartridge was first introduced in 1887. It was designed by J. Stevens Arms & Tool Company and is one of the most common ammunition calibers in the world.

It is of a relatively low cost and accommodates a low recoil, which is why it is very popular with those just starting out in pistol shooting sports. It is accepted for use in Steel Challenge

(SCSA), but not in USPSA. Due to the small caliber of the bullet, the round does not make the minor power factor needed in USPSA competition.

Rimfire cases are straight-walled and acquired their name due to the primer being built into the rim of the case. Bullet sizes run between 20 to 60 grains.

Reloading

Many long-time competitors spend time and money to perfect loads. When you are just starting out, you want to stay focused on being safe and learning the sport. Later, when you are comfortable with competing, you can take all that saved brass and start developing your own custom bullet loads.

SUMMARY

- Know the minimum round count needed for your competitive event so you can bring enough extra rounds to complete the match.
- Only use ammunition that meets the firearm manufacturer's specification for your gun.
- Try several types of ammunition and bullet weights to see how it can affect the firearm's timing and felt recoil to determine what you like best.

CHAPTER 15
SHOT TIMERS AND JOURNALS

A shot timer and a journal are important tools that allow you to become a better shooting competitor. The timer shows you how you're doing, and the journal helps you record your progress.

Breaking Things Down

It's easier to improve your overall performance by breaking down the movements and activities that take the most time. This is where shot timers become invaluable. When you improve your performance (even marginally) in several little ways, your overall performance and scores improve.

When using shot timers, ask yourself these three questions:

- Where are you spending the most time executing a skill or drill?
- Where can you reduce time by improving your skills and efficiencies?
- Where do you need to improve (based on recording previous times)?

How Shot Timers Work

Shot timers use microphones to detect your shots and record performance times. A loud beep signals the start and recording of shots. When you have finished shooting, you can review the recorded timing of your activity. These are useful in competition, as you can compare the times within a stage layout and identify the areas you need to work on.

Shot timers can be worn around your neck, arm or on your belt so you can access them easily. Having the timer on your person as you practice helps you hear the start signal, allows the timer's microphone to capture your shots better, and is a quick way to review your performance times.

Shot Timer

Shot Timer Features:

- **Time to first shot** - This is the duration between the start signal and the first shot on target. This is useful for measuring draw speed.
- **Split times or splits** - This refers to the duration between shots on one target. Split times are used to measure how quickly you can perform a follow-up shot on the same target.
- **Transitions** - This is the duration between shots on different targets. This is useful for evaluating the shooter's skill when moving to a new target.

- **The number of shots** - The timer records the total number of shots taken after the start signal, using the microphone to count them.
- **Total elapsed time** - This is the duration between the start signal and the final shot. This feature helps to measure the shooter's overall performance and total time on a stage.
- **Par times** - This feature is used to set a time duration using a start and stop window for completing different skills on the clock.
- **Random start** - The timer will signal you to start randomly. This helps you to develop a more competitive reaction time.

Have a Plan

To ensure efficient use of your shot timer, it's a good idea to have a plan each time you practice. For example, you may want to focus on specific skills, like timed accuracy or efficiency of movement. The shot timer will help you understand the time associated with the skill you chose to review, and your journal notes will help you understand where you are improving.

Performance Improvement

Most timers can be configured to start at random times. Random starts help you develop a better overall reaction time to audible starts. The par-time feature is a great way to practice and measure your skill performance in dry-fire or live-fire practice. When you start reducing par times in practice, you push yourself to improve specific skills so you can see where your current abilities start to break down.

Remember, it is important to record your performance times in a journal every time you practice. Reviewing previous sessions enables you to see where you have progressed and improved as a competitive shooter.

SUMMARY

- Using a shot timer and journal are essential tools to measuring your growth and progress.
- Breaking down movements and activities to understand where you can save time will go a long way toward improving your score and performance.
- Look for shot timers that have the features you need to measure first shots, splits, transitions, par times, random starts, total number of shots fired, and total elapsed time.
- Have a plan before you go to the range to practice and write it in your journal.
- Record your performance for each session and any other observations you may want to review later.

CHAPTER 16
PRACTICE TARGETS

When you first get started and head out to the range for a practice session, you want to go with a plan of what you intend to work on. You don't want to go without a plan and just fire bullets downrange. Take some targets with you so you can see and measure how well you are doing.

At the range, practice the fundamentals of stance, grip, sight picture on a target, and trigger control. The target shows you how you are doing. Record notes on how your first shots went, and where your follow-up shots patterned on the target. Reviewing the target for patterns will help you understand what you need to work on to improve your skills and get better at the game.

Steel vs. Cardboard

When you've become more involved in the sport, you may want to purchase a set of steel targets. Steel targets are great, as they give you instant feedback and save you time on resetting. Steel targets can help keep your practice sessions interesting. However, cardboard and paper targets allow you to see, record, and diagnose what skills need additional work. Did your shots go where you placed them? Do you need to adjust your sights, your sight picture, or your grip? Do you need to work on just pulling the trigger straight back?

SUMMARY

- Targets help you measure accuracy, and accuracy is an important aspect for all shooting sports.
- As you practice your technique, watch how it affects your performance on targets.
- Analyze what the targets tell you about where you aimed and where the shots impacted across different distances, transitions, and shot order.

For additional material on practice targets, see the companion website at

https://pistolshootingsports.com/book-bonus.

PART IV
PISTOL SHOOTING FUNDAMENTALS

CHAPTER 17
OVERVIEW AND TRAINING

OVERVIEW

As with any sport, you need to focus first on the fundamentals so you can build your skills on a solid foundation of good technique and best practices. Pistol shooting sports are about accuracy and speed. When you start out, focus on one thing at a time and ensure you have mastered the concept before moving on.

I recommend that you start with fundamentals and build on success. This all relates to your stance, grip, sight picture, and trigger control. You want to develop a good understanding of what it takes to be consistent and demonstrate accuracy through proper skills.

After you master and demonstrate consistent fundamentals, your speed will follow. Speed is not just doing what you know faster; it is a combination of doing things sooner and more efficiently.

Remove any unnecessary movement or extra dependencies that over complicate your movements. If you over complicate with head moves, knee bends, or shoulder shrugs, it will just be harder to repeat these actions. Just stay relaxed and focus on the basics before you begin.

Think only about getting a good grip on the gun when drawing it out of the holster, seeing the target and bringing the firearm to your eye, and feeling the trigger wall before you break the shot. Don't distract yourself with other thoughts or ideas. Keep it simple, take breaks, apply focus, and it will happen.

TRAINING

Like any skill, pistol shooting requires a lot of practice and attention in order to improve. Training with an instructor is one of the fastest ways to increase your skills. A class can cover a lot in a fixed period of time. You will want to record what you learned from each training drill, how to set it up for practice later, and how the drill can improve your skills. Take notes or record as much information as you can for review later. Online resources and books can be done at your own pace, so it helps to set a schedule that allows you to focus on a different concept per training session. The best competitors create a training schedule, plan their training sessions, and stick to their plans.

Take Notes and Have a Plan

For instructor-led classes, I recommend outlining the topics covered and sketching diagrams of drills. It is useful to highlight any of your own insights, the instructor's contact information, and the contact information of other classmates. Instructor-led classes are a great way to meet new friends who share a similar interest in the sport.

It's good to have an idea of what you want to work on as you engage in training and before you go to the range. Write down the things you want to work on for your training session, then test and record your performance so you can review it later.

Having a plan before each practice session will help you focus and progress quickly rather than just showing up and shooting bullets.

Write the date and the purpose of the practice session in your training journal. Make a note of the questions you want answers to before you head out, so you can record your findings during the session. Write down what you learned and want to remember. Often, this will lead you to write down more questions that you can pursue in other practice sessions.

Logging performance times allows you to review your progress as you improve. Other things to include: the date, location, firearm used, ammunition used, drills undertaken, a sketch of the setup you worked on, approximate number of rounds, performance times for draws, splits, transitions, and accuracy. Some people write notes around what they observed in themselves, what they learned, and what they would like to work on next.

Video Recordings

Video recordings are a great way to identify areas of performance where you are doing well and where you need to improve. Recording simple videos with your smartphone will allow you to capture practice sessions and match performances that you can review later. If you do not have someone to record you during your next practice session, bring a tripod and record yourself. At matches, have someone record your stage runs and then record other competitors for a comparison. Reviewing other competitors' runs will allow you to evaluate stage plans, execution, and overall performance. You can incorporate what you learn into your next practice session. You will start to see how the best competitors execute smoother, do things sooner, and make fewer mistakes.

SUMMARY

- An effective training plan is about decomposing the thing you want to work on down to its smallest parts.
- Keep a training journal and record video of yourself.
- Review your notes and recordings as you create training plans for skills you want to improve.
- Look back over your notes from time to time. This will reinforce your progress.

CHAPTER 18
EYE DOMINANCE AND TESTING

Your dominant eye is the eye your brain prefers for processing sight information. You need to know which eye your brain prefers so you can position the gun's sights for your dominant eye. This usually happens unconsciously without much thought, as your brain already knows which eye it trusts. Why do we need to know which eye the brain trusts? Because it will help you and your brain be more accurate and consistent at speed.

Two-thirds of the population are right-eye dominant, and one-third is left-eye dominant. A few people have no eye dominance, so you will want to check and understand which type you are.

How to Test for Eye Dominance

Pick an object that is around seven yards away and about the size of a doorknob or light switch. Bring both hands up and form a triangle window that frames the object. With both eyes open, extend your arms, keeping the object or target centered inside the triangle window. Next, close each eye one at a time and hold your triangle window in the same position without moving it. Start by closing your left eye and noting what you see. Then open your left eye and close your right eye, noting what you see. Whatever open eye you saw the object framed inside your hands is the one your brain trusts the most. This would be your dominant eye.

Right Eye Dominant

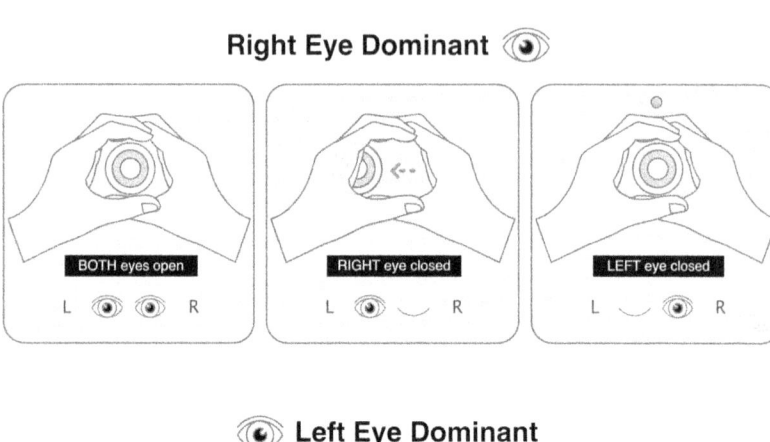

Left Eye Dominant

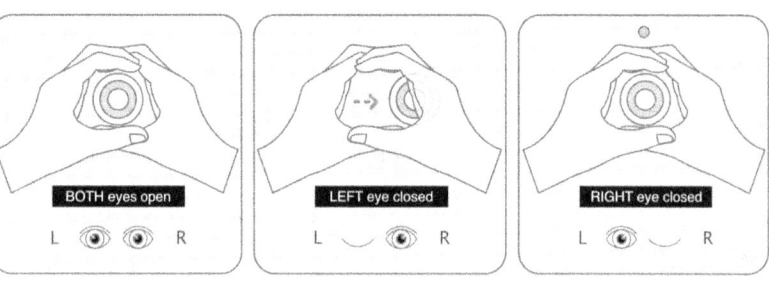

Eye Dominance Testing

You can do these tests under different conditions and at different distances to see what your brain prefers, so that when you mount your gun and form a sight picture, you can do it quickly and accurately.

SUMMARY

- Your dominant eye is the eye your brain prefers for processing sight information.
- You need to know which eye your brain prefers so you can position the gun's sights effectively.
- Test your eye dominance at different distances using the outline above.

CHAPTER 19
SIGHTS AND ALIGNMENT

Sight picture is critical because it brings together three crucial elements: your eyes, the sights, and the target. Your sight picture is what you need to see through the sights on a target to make an accurate shot. It consistently tells you where the shot is going to hit the target when you pull the trigger straight back.

Iron Sight Alignment

Sight alignment is the orientation of the gun's front and rear sights to each other. Your sight alignment tells you what adjustments are needed to achieve the best shot on target. Proper sight alignment will translate into better sight pictures and accuracy.

Iron Sight Alignment

A proper sight alignment will position the front post directly in the middle of the notch of the rear sight, and both front and rear sights should be level, or appear to be the same height, as you look through them. You may have already heard the saying "equal height, equal light," which is a quick way to think about proper sight alignment.

Holds and Points of Impact

Depending on how your firearm's point of aim is configured, how you create your pistol's sight picture will be different in order to achieve the desired point of impact. If you have adjustable sights, you can set them to the type of hold you prefer.

- **Six O'clock Hold** - After you line up your sights, the front sight should be sitting below the target. This is also referred to as a lollipop or "pumpkin on a post," where the front sight is the post.
- **Top of the Blade** - After you line up your sights, the top of the blade splits the target horizontally, so your shots hit just above your front sight. This is sometimes called a center mass hold for combat accuracy at ten to fifteen yards.
- **Cover Hold** - After you line up your sights, the front sight's dot covers the point of impact.

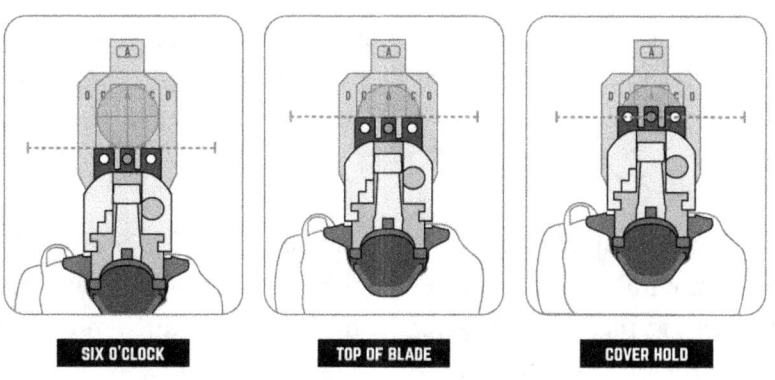

Holds and Points of Impact

For competitive shooting, the top of blade or center mass hold is recommended as a place to start because it allows you to see more of the target. It also allows you to quickly see where the shots are going and is more precise than the six o'clock hold. Visually splitting targets in half with a top of blade hold works on any-sized target over varying distances. This makes it more consistent and quicker to train your eyes.

Eye Focus

Start with your stance and focus squarely on the target. Bring the gun up, keeping your head straight, and view the sight alignment as the pistol moves over the target in line with your dominant eye. Check your eyes' focus as it shifts to the front sight. Focusing on the front sight is a quick way to begin building consistency around your sight picture. If your sights stay aligned as you press the trigger, you can group your shots on the target. The key is not to disturb a good sight picture as you break the shot. At close range, you may find you can be less precise and still score reasonable hits, but the farther the target is, the more you will need a good sight picture and trigger technique.

When you are focused more on the target than the sights, you may start to lose sight alignment and become less aware of where your front sight is. Test this by taking three shots using front sight focus, then three shots with target focus from different distances. The longer the shot, the better the sight picture and technique that is needed.

Iron Sight Adjustment

If you have adjustable sights, you want to have consistent data to work with before you begin making adjustments. Use a prop as a resting platform to increase stability and reduce movement as you review and make adjustments. For example, a bench rest, sandbag, or your shooting bag can help your testing and ensure adjustments are consistent. Each competitor sees things a little differently, so find what works for you.

Start at five to seven yards so you can see the point of aim (POA) and point of impact (POI) quickly. You will be fine-tuning at farther distances after you confirm how things work at shorter ones. Most pistols come bore-sighted from the factory and won't be noticeably off at shorter distances. Check the horizontal adjustment first before you move on to any vertical elevation changes.

Horizontal Adjustments (Left and Right)

If your shots are impacting to the left of where you are aiming, you will need to adjust your rear sight to the right. If they are impacting to the right of where you are aiming, you will adjust the rear sight to the left.

Vertical Adjustment (Up and Down)

If your shots are impacting higher than your point of aim, you will need to lower your rear sight. If your shots are impacting lower than your point of aim, you will need to raise your rear sight.

Remember, for horizontal and vertical adjustments, move the rear sight in the direction you need to correct for. These adjustments do not change how the gun shoots, but they do align your point of aim and point of impact to be in the same place.

Take your time and make a small adjustment in one direction at a time. Test your change with at least three shots to confirm the point of aim (POA) and point of impact (POI). When your shots start to align where your sights say they should, increase the distance to the target and test again. Move out to ten, fifteen, and twenty yards and follow the same process to fine-tune your adjustments and determine how your pistol performs at different distances. As you test your sights at distances, the horizontal adjustment should stay consistent, but the vertical elevation can change depending on how far you are from the target. Knowing how your pistol will perform at different distances will improve your ability to choose the best sight picture before you take a shot.

But what if you don't have adjustable sights? You can perform the same tests at different distances using the same process. You will want to observe how your pistol performs and know what sight alignment is needed at each distance to make good shots. If your shots don't consistently line up on target with proper sight alignment, you may want to have a trained gunsmith take a look to determine where adjustments can be made. You can also talk to them about adding an adjustable sight if you need it.

Sight Picture on the Move

As you start to practice your skills, try shooting with both eyes open. You will still use your dominant eye to validate the sight picture as needed. Start at five yards and increase the distance as you train yourself to see what is needed. This technique will help you see faster during transitions, acquire targets quicker, and help you position the gun where your eyes are focused. If you practice this way, your brain will become comfortable knowing how to trust and read sight pictures faster. As you increase distance on targets, you will see that staying focused on the front sight with your dominant eye and having a good sight picture is imperative. Take the time to understand what you need to be seeing before you take the shot.

Red Dot Sights

Red dot sights are becoming more and more popular in shooting sports competitions. Sight pictures are simplified when using a red dot system because you only need to see the dot on the target. Red dots allow you to stay "target focused" as you move from target to target. The benefits of using red dot sights allow for simplified sight pictures and faster target acquisition.

One big difference between a red dot and iron sight system is the height distance from the sight (or dot) to the barrel's bore axis. Most iron sights sit low to the bore axis, so they can be more consistent across near to far distances, whereas red dots sit higher. The accuracy of any sighting system must support the intersection of the sights and the barrel to the target.

Red Dot Sight Adjustment

Point of aim (POA) is where the red dot appears on the target as you aim the pistol. Point of impact (POI) is where the bullet impacts the target using a consistent aiming point. Sighting in a red dot, or "zeroing," is making the POA align with the POI at a given distance.

Red dots use a consistent measurement called "minutes of angle" (MOA) to align your POA to the POI. An MOA represents 1.047 inches at 100 yards. We will round 1.047 inches to 1.0 inch for our pistol example below.

How the Math Works

If your red dot's POA is on the bullseye at 100 yards and your bullet impacts approximately three inches to the right of where you aimed, you would adjust the dot three MOA to the left. This would align the point of aim with the point of impact. (Refer to your red dot sight manual for details on how MOA increments are measured for your sight adjustments.)

I do *not* recommend sighting in your pistol at 100 yards. The average target distance for USPSA and SCSA is less than thirty-five yards. It is recommended that you start at ten yards so you can see the target, keep the math simple, and then confirm your settings at further distances. *Note: Your final zero will be somewhere between fifteen and twenty-five yards.*

- 100 yards = 1-inch adjustment = 1 MOA
- 10 yards = 1-inch adjustment = 10 MOAs
- 10 yards = ½-inch adjustment = 5 MOAs

How to sight in your pistol using a dot sight

Overview - Adjust and confirm your settings at ten yards. This makes it easy to see, easy to adjust, and easy to do the math. The next step is to test your settings across several distances to see how the POI height changes. Adjust the horizontal only as need to keep it in the center of the target. The last step is to choose a distance that represents an average target distance for the competitions you will be shooting. Pick a distance between fifteen and twenty-five yards to start. Make the final vertical adjustments at your chosen distance, then confirm your POI at several distances so you know how it will perform. Below is a summary of the five steps.

1. Test and adjust POA/POI at ten yards.
2. Test settings at fifteen, twenty, and twenty-five yards and adjust horizontal POI as needed.
3. Test and adjust vertical POA/POI using an average target distance (for example, seventeen yards).
4. Review and confirm POA/POI settings at three, five, ten, fifteen, twenty, and twenty-five yards.
5. Test your settings in several practice sessions to determine what works best for you.

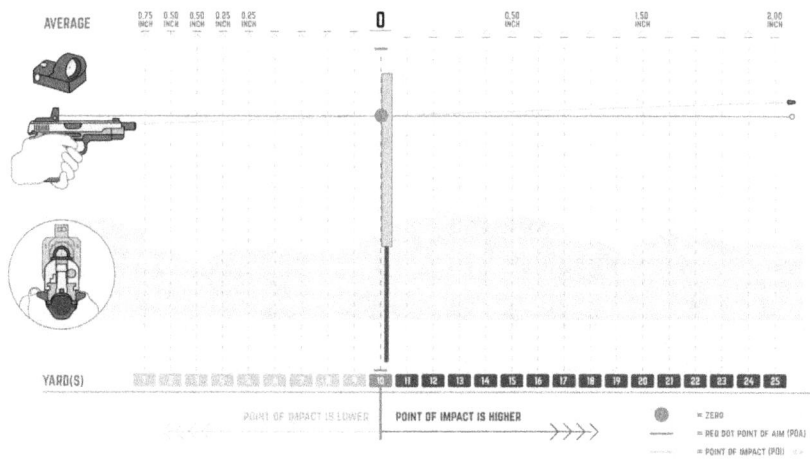

10 Yard Zero

1. Test and adjust POA/POI at ten yards - Start at ten yards and adjust your red dot to its smallest size so you can refine your aiming point. You will be shooting three to five rounds for each test. You want your shots to group as much as possible. It is recommended that you use targets with a clear one-inch center point for aiming. Targets with one- to half-inch lines will help you adjust the zero quicker. Use the same ammunition you will compete with for consistent results.

The objective is to make consistent shots, taking as much time as you need. Practice good trigger control, aiming for consistent, accurate shots. Start at ten yards and sight your pistol's dot on the center of your target, take three to five shots, then inspect your group and adjust your sights' horizontal and vertical MOAs as needed.

2. Test settings at fifteen, twenty, and twenty-five yards and adjust horizontal POI as needed - Only adjust the horizontal at this stage. You will start to notice differences in POI elevation as you shoot the targets at each distance. The farther the distance, the higher the POI. This difference is normal.

3. Test and adjust vertical POA/POI using an average target distance - Choose an average distance for targets you will be shooting the most in your type of competition (see targets and distances below). Pick a distance between fifteen and twenty yards and set up your target. At this point, the horizontal settings should be accurate, and you will only be focused on the vertical elevation adjustment.

Tip: To quickly measure vertical settings at different distances, I like to place a line of blue painters' tape on a target and fire several shots at the tape. You can quickly measure how high or low the POI is from the original line of tape.

4. Review and confirm POA/POI settings at three, five, ten, fifteen, twenty, and twenty-five yards - The closer target's POI will be a little low, and the farthest target's will be a little higher than your zeroed distance. You want to know how your pistol performs at each distance so you won't be second-guessing where the POI is during a match.

5. Test your settings in several practice sessions to determine what works best for you - Set up a sample stage with targets at varying distances and check your performance. You can quickly change your POA/POI using different distances to zero because you only need to change the vertical setting at the new distance.

Targets and Distances

Steel challenge - The farthest target distance is a large steel rectangle at thirty-five yards, and the closest targets are at seven yards. The smallest targets are ten-inch disks at eighteen yards and twelve-inch disks at twenty yards. If you know you need to aim at the center or lower on far targets, this will help your performance because knowing where your pistol shoots at a range of distances is important. If you sight it in at fifteen yards, you will be a little high at thirty-five yards and a little low at seven yards, but you may not even notice, as you should be on target throughout the entire range.

USPSA - In USPSA, the range of distances will be different based on each stage design. For close targets, I recommend practicing on a cardboard A-zone headbox at three to five feet so you can determine where you need to aim in order to hit the center. For longer distances, you can set up a steel target at twenty-five, thirty-five, or even fifty yards and quickly confirm your settings.

Where is the dot?

One of the biggest adjustments when moving from iron sights to a red dot is to make sure you have the right index on the gun. You want to bring the gun up and immediately see a dot on target. If you are switching from iron sights, it is common to see competitors rotate the gun until they see the dot. This is usually caused by having the gun too low.

Practice bringing the gun all the way up to your eye level until you see the dot. You can build a good index by practicing your draw to a target in dry-fire. It is helpful to think about bringing the gun all the way up to eye level instead of just up as you draw and practice. Start with both eyes open and align your stance squarely with the target. Bring the gun up to eye level, keeping your head straight until you see the dot appear on the target. You will find that if you don't get a good grip, your dot index will be inconsistent. Ensure you are gripping the gun in the same way each time as you practice.

SUMMARY

- A good sight picture brings your eyes and the gun's sights on target in a consistent manner so you can make predictable shots.
- In order to maximize your accuracy, understand your firearm's point of aim and point of impact so you can adjust sights or holds to deliver consistent shots.
- Test your firearm at different distances to confirm your sights' settings and accuracy.

CHAPTER 20
GRIP AND TRIGGER CONTROL

Your grip and trigger control are instrumental in determining how accurately you are going to be able to shoot at speed. You want to consistently execute building your grip from the draw so that you don't need to think about the mechanics of the movement. You will want to start slowly with the fundamentals and build on proper techniques.

BUILDING YOUR GRIP

Semi-Auto

Dominant Hand:

1 - Keep the web of your hand high on the back strap, or beavertail, of the pistol.

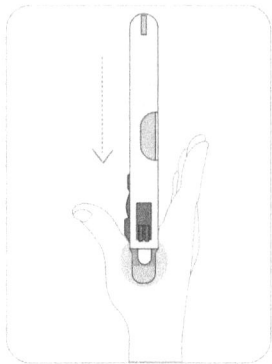

Figure 1

2 - All three fingers under the trigger guard should be touching with the middle finger as high as possible on the front strap. There should be no space between the bottom of the trigger guard and your three fingers.

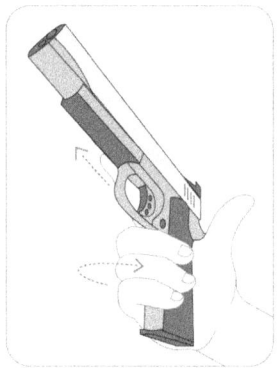

Figure 2

Your trigger finger should be pointing in the same direction as the barrel, down the side of the gun, outside the trigger guard. Your trigger finger must stay outside the trigger guard until you are ready to fire. The thumb on your dominant hand must remain up and ready to overlap your support hand after it is on the pistol.

Support Hand:

3 - All four fingers should fit under the trigger guard and be placed as high as possible.

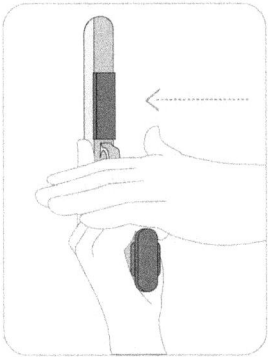

Figure 3

4 - Your palm will fit on the side of the pistol, just behind your dominant hand's fingertips, maximizing the contact area against the pistol's grips.

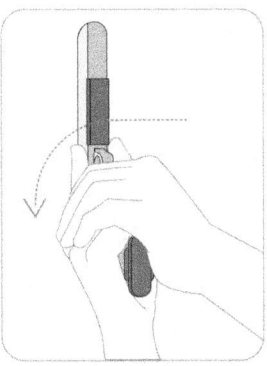

Figure 4

You want to minimize any open space toward the back of your hands, so they are both touching.

• • •

5 - Rotate your support hand's wrist so your thumb is pointing in the same direction as your pistol's barrel. The four fingers on your support hand will now be angled toward the ground. Your support hand fingers wrap around your dominant hand to establish your grip side to side.

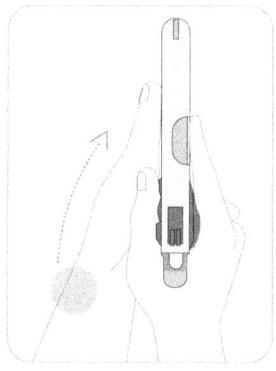

Figure 5

Extend both arms using the proper grip to create a triangle between your two arms and chest. Recoil control should be supported by your arms instead of your wrists. Using the right techniques will help you control recoil better, so the gun returns to the same location every time.

Grip Pressure: The grip pressure of the dominant hand works front to back, whereas your support hand pressure works side to side. Use as much grip pressure as you can with your support hand. Try flexing your muscles instead of tensing them to the point of shaking. When you flex your larger muscle groups to create more pressure side to side, this will create more stability as your palms press together.

Your dominant hand grip should be strong enough to hold the gun and ensure your trigger finger can work the trigger without disrupting your sight picture. You can test your dominant hand grip by watching your sights as you pull the trigger straight back. If you introduce movement as you pull the trigger, ensure you are pulling the trigger straight back, then adjust your grip and try again.

Your grip should support pulling the trigger as independently as possible. You don't want the pressure of your grip overriding the execution of the trigger. When you have a good grip, the sights will move smoothly straight up and down through recoil instead of in random directions.

Remember, as you practice your gripping technique, you want to bring your hands together and present them at the same level as your eyes. Your elbows should be angled toward the ground, not pointing out to the side.

Take time to test what works best for you and your firearm. If you have sweaty hands or it's hot where you shoot, you may want to add grip tape to your pistol or use grip enhancer on your hands to help increase your ability to maintain grip adhesion.

Revolver

Dominant Hand:

Revolvers use the same technique outlined above with some minor differences.

1 - Keep the web of your hand high on the back of the pistol's grip.

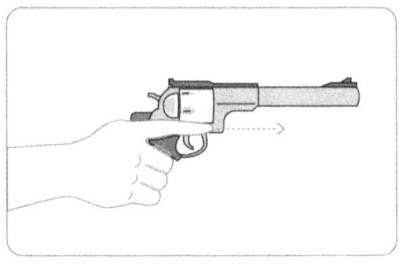

Figure 1

2 - All three fingers under the trigger guard should be touching with the middle finger as high as possible under the trigger guard. Your trigger finger should be pointing down the side of the revolver, outside the trigger guard. Your trigger finger must stay outside the trigger guard until you are ready to fire.

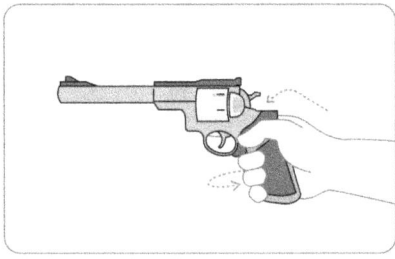

Figure 2

The thumb on your dominant hand will wrap around and tuck in against the grip.

Support Hand:

3 - All four fingers should be under the trigger guard as high as possible. Position your nondominant thumb on top of your strong hand's thumb.

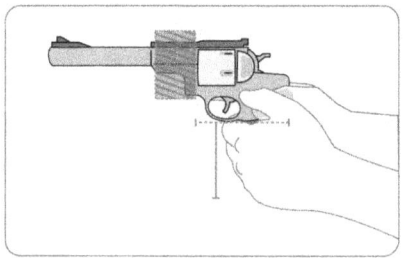

Figure 3 & 4

Important: Do not place fingers anywhere near the front of the cylinder on a revolver. Hot gasses and high pressures are released as you fire each shot, and they can burn or damage fingers.

4 - Your palm will fit on the side of the pistol, just behind your dominant hand's fingertips, maximizing the contact area against the revolver's grips. You want to minimize any open space toward the back of your hands, so they are both touching. Keep your fingers off the cylinder so that it may rotate freely as you pull the trigger.

TRIGGER CONTROL

Managing your trigger is a fundamental skill when it comes to pistol shooting sports. It is one of the most critical aspects of a pistol competitor's skill and performance. It is recommended that you practice trigger control in dry-fire with a safe firearm where no ammunition is present. Trigger control is all about actuating the trigger with the least amount of influence on the pistol and sight picture. Trigger control starts with proper grip, trigger finger placement, and moving through the four stages of prep, wall, break, and reset.

Trigger Finger Placement

The best way to build an understanding of the techniques used in trigger control and finger placement starts in dry-fire. Make sure you are working with an unloaded firearm in a safe location with no ammunition present.

Trigger finger placement is all about finding the right place for your index finger on the trigger so you can accurately place shots consistently. The best position is one in which when you press, you can feel all four stages of the trigger transition and the movement does not influence the shot negatively. Understand that to find the best placement, you will need to start with proper grip and test the positions that work best for you and your selected pistol.

Example

Check that you are working with an unloaded firearm, in a safe location, and with no ammunition present. Start by gripping the pistol as high as you can with your dominant hand. Place your index finger down the side of the gun out of the trigger guard and be sure that the web of your hand is high on the back of the pistol.

This placement will help you create the grip you need to manage recoil. Wrap the rest of your fingers around the grip, holding it firmly in your hand. You should feel the back strap of the gun firmly pressed against your palm.

Place your index finger on the trigger so that the pad of your finger rests naturally on the trigger's face. The idea is to connect your finger with the trigger so you can press back without disrupting the sight picture.

If you insert your trigger finger too far, it will pull the gun's point of aim in the direction of your dominant hand. If you don't have enough of your finger covering the trigger as you press, it will push toward your support hand.

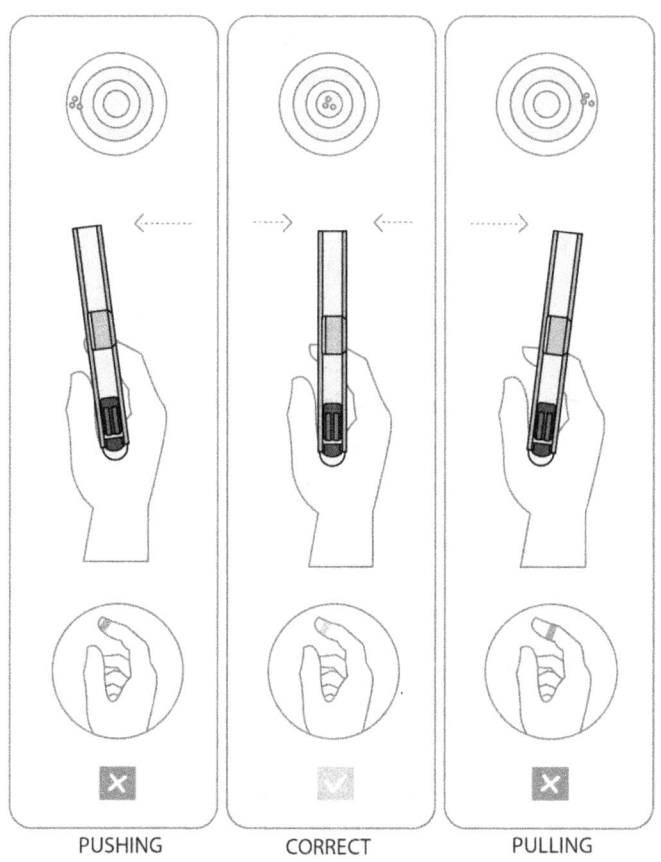

Trigger Finger Placement

Try inserting your finger farther than required so you can observe what happens as you press the trigger and the pistol moves. Now test what happens when you move your finger out, using only the tip of your finger. Now adjust the placement of your trigger finger to the location that disrupts the pistol the least as you pull the trigger straight back. For most people, this will be the first pad of your finger pressing against the center of the trigger. Take note of where you feel the pressure of the trigger on your finger and where it works best.

Depending on the type of trigger you have, you may notice it feels heavier when your finger is higher on the trigger face and lighter when it is lower. The best location is the one you can consistently find where you don't disrupt the sight picture as you pull the trigger through its full travel.

Trigger Press Stages

A trigger press is broken down into four stages. It is important to understand each step and how it works on your firearm. Understanding how it feels will be different for every firearm—even similar models from the same manufacturer will feel different. Be sure your trigger finger placement is consistent as you move through the four stages so you notice how different they feel.

Four Stages:

- **Prep** - Take up the trigger's slack.
- **Wall** - The end of prep, which is the last point of travel before the shot is fired.
- **Break** - Hammer or firing pin is released and gun fires.
- **Reset** - Trigger moves forward to enable another cycle.

Prep - This is the part of the trigger pull where you are taking up the slack or prepping the trigger before you break the shot. It should feel relatively light as you move through the pretravel. When shooting for accuracy, remove as much of the pretravel as you can before breaking a shot. Prepping the trigger in this way minimizes the disruption to your sight picture before you break the shot.

Wall - This is where you feel the most resistance when pressing the trigger. As you move through the pretravel, it will start to feel stiffer and reach a maximum weight of feedback against your trigger finger. The feedback wall tells you when you are at the end of pretravel. Learning where to stop and feel the wall will help you improve your accuracy. The next step is to apply just enough pressure to break through the wall and fire the pistol.

Break - This is where you fire the shot, and the hammer or firing pin is released. The break should have just enough pressure to fire the pistol and not slam through the wall when firing a shot. In some cases, the break may catch you by surprise the first few times you practice. Get a feel for how much pressure is needed to move through the wall and break the shot.

Reset - This is where you release pressure on the trigger so it can move forward and reset the pistol to fire the next shot. You should observe how far you need to move your trigger finger forward to achieve the reset. Sometimes pistols will have an audible click or tactile feedback you can feel as it resets. After the trigger has reset, the cycle is complete, and you are back to prep.

Remember that every firearm—and every trigger—will feel different. Where you place your finger on the trigger will change the feeling of pressure needed to break the shot. Be consistent with your trigger finger placement so you can build on your skill and performance.

Things to Avoid:

1. Pinning the trigger - This is where you follow the first three steps—prep, wall, and break—but instead of releasing and resetting, you keep the trigger back, or pin it to the rear of its full travel. (Note: When you pin a trigger, you are exerting force on the pistol, and this will disrupt the sight picture and cause the point of aim to dip.)

Be aware that if you do this at speed, your shots may hit lower than where you are aiming, and this may slow your ability to execute follow-up shots due to the added motion and the reset taking longer to complete. To avoid pinning the trigger, practice using just enough pressure to break the shot, then start your reset.

2. Slapping the trigger - This is where you pull through the full trigger action in one motion without feeling the prep, wall, or break. Slapping allows you to fire several shots quickly, but your accuracy will suffer, as the slamming of the trigger will move your sight picture and negatively influence where your shots go.

SUMMARY

- Building the proper grip and executing good trigger control will determine how accurately you can shoot at speed.
- Practice building your grip using good technique, taking notice of your dominant hand and support hand positions.
- Check the grip pressure of your dominant hand and ensure it does not negatively influence the sight picture as you actuate the trigger. Apply firm support-hand pressure side to side and adjust both hands' grip pressure to achieve best results.
- Practice trigger control in dry-fire in a safe location with a safe firearm where no ammunition is present.
- Check your finger placement on the trigger for the best position that does not negatively influence the sight picture when you pull straight back.

CHAPTER 21
BREATHING, STANCE, AND RECOIL CONTROL

BREATHING

Breathing is something we do unconsciously every day. Try this test to see the impact breathing has on your ability to aim:

Extend both arms in front of you, keeping your shoulders square. Make a fist with your dominant hand and point with your index finger at a point of reference or target that is five yards away. Use your supportive hand to wrap the fist of your dominant hand. Rotate the thumb on your supportive hand so that your dominant hand's index finger and support hand's thumb point in the same direction. Inhale and exhale a few times and see how it changes where you are pointing your fingers.

For most people, your pointing finger will rise and fall for each breath. For short-range targets, this may not seem like a big deal, but for long-range targets, breathing and minimizing movement is essential. Try looking at a target that is fifteen to twenty-five yards away and do the same test. You will quickly observe how this influences your accuracy.

Slowing your breath and getting the perfect sight picture before you break the shot will allow you to settle in and make accurate shots at distance. But what do you do when you are expected to take multiple shots at speed while moving? You will want to learn how and where to breathe, move, and execute good fire control that supports consistent performance. When you don't breathe consistently, your heart rate will rise, and you will begin to breathe faster to get it back down.

Combining breathing control with trigger control for the best results

The best time to take that hard shot is during what is called the "respiratory pause." The pause refers to when you have taken a breath and then exhaled. Toward the bottom of the exhale, you are the most relaxed and will have the least disruption to your sight picture—this is the best time to take a difficult shot.

You can extend the respiratory pause a few seconds if needed. Start by focusing on the sight picture and prepping the trigger at the start of your exhale so that when you are most relaxed (toward the end), you can break the shot and continue normal breathing. Proper breathing will help increase the overall accuracy of your shooting as well as keep your brain and body oxygenated as you compete. Failing to breathe properly will cause you to experience a lack of focus and changes in your vision.

STANCE

Your stance is the foundational platform that will help you to become an effective competitor. A proper stance will support you in absorbing recoil, shooting accurately at speed, and driving efficient movement.

Face the target with your whole body. Make your hips and shoulders parallel to the area where you will be shooting. Start with your feet spread at or slightly wider than shoulder width, then place one foot back—start at about half of your foot's length. If you are right-handed, stagger your right foot back, and if you are left-handed, stagger your left foot. You will know you are in the correct position if you can draw a line from the tip of your rear foot and it divides the instep of your forward foot.

Your feet can point slightly outward, with your weight equally distributed. Drop your butt and bend your knees slightly so you can shift your weight and flex easily from this stance. Bending your knees and dropping your butt also helps you create a lower center of gravity, which allows you to absorb recoil and shift weight quickly where needed.

Check where you feel the pressure on the bottoms of your feet. Is it forward on your toes or backward on your heels? Bend forward slightly at the waist, keeping your back straight. You should feel more weight on the front of your feet. If you did this in front of a mirror, you would see your shoulders slightly in front of your hips. This stance is a good starting point to work with. The goal is to be comfortable, absorb recoil, and move efficiently.

Keep your arms straight and bring your hands together with arms extended in front of your body. Point forward with both of your thumbs at eye level as you form a triangle with your arms and chest. Lean forward slightly, keeping your back straight. Look at your hands with both eyes open, facing forward, and keep your head straight. Do not tilt your head left or right. Keep your shoulders relaxed, lock your elbows, then relax them just enough so they are not tense. You should feel the difference in tension between "locked" and "nearly locked." Most people feel more comfortable when their elbows are fully extended and nearly locked, as this allows for a stable platform and proper transmission of recoil to the rest of your body.

Test your stance without a firearm by having someone apply pressure on your hands when they are out in front of you. You can test this by yourself using a wall or post. You want to feel the pressure on your hands and keep the triangle you formed with your upper body straight. Adjust your shoulders so your arms can be supported comfortably. You want to firmly flex larger muscle groups rather than tensing them as you feel the pressure. Adjust to what gives you the best results. Remember to stay relaxed as you adjust and flex muscle groups to find the best combination.

Practice moving your head and eyes from target to target and bring your hands to where your eyes are focused. Use your legs and larger muscle groups to begin moving, and your arms and hands will follow. As you practice this technique, you will notice it takes less effort to drive the gun smoothly from target to target.

Adjusting to a more aggressive stance to support higher recoil and movement

When you need to adjust to a more aggressive stance, move your rear foot farther back and increase the weight on the balls of your feet. Drop your butt and bend your knees more as you lean forward. This creates an even stronger position from front to back and side to side. The more you can practice and develop your stance, the faster you will find what works best for you.

RECOIL CONTROL

Recoil is when the gun's muzzle moves up and down or rocks in your hand as you break the shot. Recoil control, done correctly, should allow the gun to return to the same sight picture you saw before breaking the shot. This is essential because that is what allows you to shoot at speed. You want the muzzle of the pistol to travel in an up-and-down motion, and your grip needs to eliminate as much side-to-side movement as possible. Grip technique and stance will determine how your gun behaves after you break the shot. The better your technique, the quicker you will be able to recover after the shot and be ready for the next one.

Recoil control can only be tested when you shoot live ammunition and can watch the sights' lift and return. Recoil from the gun will expose any weak areas in your grip and stance. This feedback tells you how well everything is working. Watch the front sight, or dot, lift as you break the shot. See how they track. Did the sight return to the original position or something else? Review your grip technique and try slight variations so you can see what influences a quicker return of the original sight picture on target.

Bullet Loads

It is recommended that you try different cartridges with different bullet weights to see how they cycle your gun and introduce higher or lower felt recoil. In 9mm, you should try 115-, 124-, and 147-grain bullets. In a .40 S&W, try 165-, 180-, and 200-grain bullets. You will feel the difference in recoil and observe how quickly your gun cycles with different loads.

The larger the bullet weight or grain, the less powder is used to achieve the right pressure to cycle and fire the bullet. The less snappy the cartridges load, the slower the gun cycles, and the lower the felt recoil. You may perceive this difference when you use smaller grain bullets, as they can use more powder and cause the gun's timing to feel snappier in your hand.

Refining your technique and follow-through

Start by setting up a target at five to seven yards. Fire one shot and observe if your sights return to the original aiming point. At shorter distances, you should see the sights lift and return to where the bullet impacted the target. Adjust your grip and stance until the sights return to the original aiming point and sight picture. Try this several times until you consistently see the sights return to where you started.

When you are comfortable with your single-shot technique, add a second shot to the drill. As the gun is returning from the recoil of the first shot, see your sights return on target, prep the trigger, and take a second shot. You want to maintain good recoil control so you can execute the second shot at speed. Make sure you are not just slapping the trigger to get the second shot. Take the time to see the sights lift, return, prep the trigger, and then take the second shot.

When you are consistent with your first and second shot, you can start to add additional shots, working your way up to a total of six. You want all of your shots to group on the target, so take your time and build up your technique. Multiple consistent shots may take some practice at first, but it will give you the feedback you need to adjust and see results quickly.

When you can consistently place six shots, time yourself and review the total time for all six. You are only looking to review the time between each shot and how accurately you placed each shot. As you start to improve, you can increase the distance to ten, twelve, or fifteen yards. You may take longer to see each shot at the longer distances, and this is normal. The main thing is to work on being consistent. Be sure to practice with the same type of ammo and loads.

SUMMARY

- Understanding how breathing can affect your shooting and knowing when to breathe will improve your accuracy at longer distances.
- A good stance will absorb recoil, drive efficient movement, and help you get your sights back on target quickly.
- Practice your athletic stance and technique to understand the right balance for you and your body composition.
- Recoil control can only be tested using live ammunition. When done correctly, the gun's sights will lift and return to the original point of aim.
- Different bullet loads will cause firearms to recoil and cycle differently, so experiment to find the ones you and your gun like the best.

CHAPTER 22
DRAWS AND RELOADING

Your draw is the skill that connects your grip to the presentation of the gun. You want to ensure good technique around your draw because that is how you start each competitive run. Take the time to focus on technique so you can build on good habits.

You want to be able to look at a target and, on signal, present the gun quickly and consistently. When practicing drawing your pistol, think about where you will finish. Draws and reloads are one of the best things to practice in dry-fire. Start by getting into your stance and looking at the first target you will engage. Your holster and pistol should be secure on your belt, in a position that is comfortable and complies with competition rules.

When practicing drawing the pistol from the holster, the two most popular starting positions are referred to as: "wrists below belt" or "wrists above shoulders," which is also called the surrender draw. The only difference between the two is where you start with your hands.

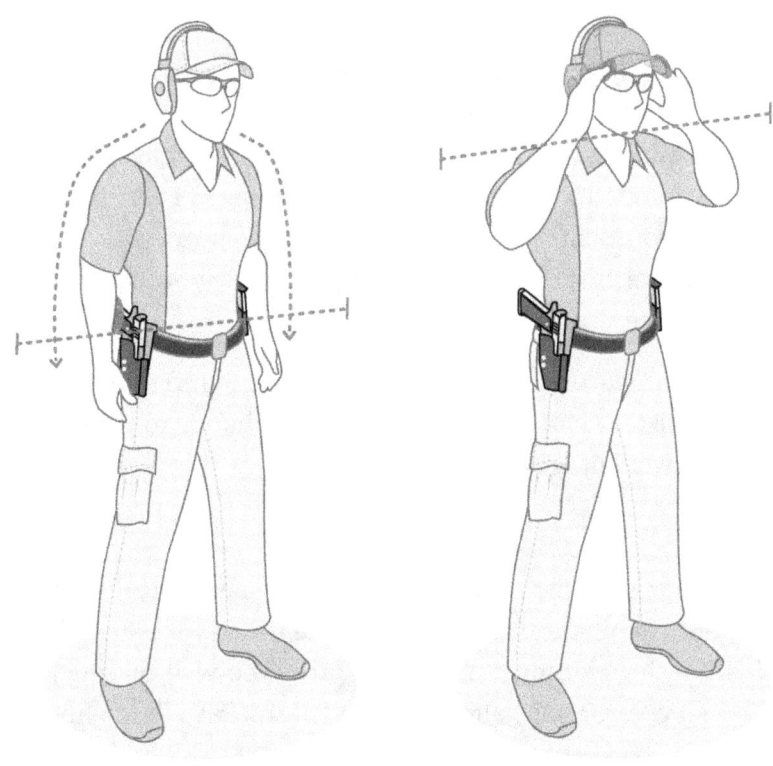

Wrists Below Belt   Wrists Above Shoulders

Wrists Below Belt

When using this type of draw, start by relaxing your arms and letting your hands fall to your sides naturally. The crease of your wrists should be below your belt.

Your dominant hand should be close to your firearm to reduce movement. It is a good idea to make some contact with the handle of the pistol with your arm as it rests at your side. Try to use the same position and touch point as an index for consistency.

• • •

Wrists Above Shoulders

When using this technique, start with the crease of your wrists above your shoulders. It is a good idea to start in the same position each time as you train. There are two recommended places for your hands to start above your shoulders. The first one is touching your hat, and the second is touching your ears or hearing protection. It does not matter which you choose—just do it the same way every time.

A consistent starting position will help you build a good index and a consistent pattern as you move your hands to the pistol in the same way with each draw.

Position 1

From either starting position, move your hands to Position 1, with your dominant hand seated on the back of the pistol's grip and riding high on the back of the gun. The web of your hand should sit comfortably, allowing your thumb and index finger to align on each side of the frame.

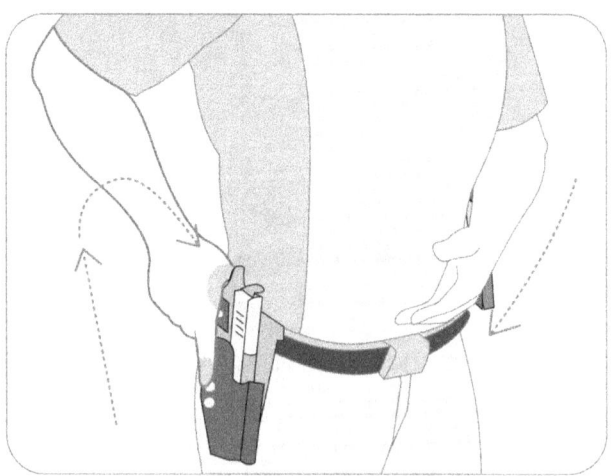

Draw - Position 1

Your grip should be as high as possible, as it will help minimize recoil and allow you to get back on target quickly. Your support hand will move to your belly button with your palm open.

Position 2

Draw the gun from the holster, ensuring you have a solid grip with your dominant hand and your index finger is in contact with the side of the gun. Do not place your finger directly into the trigger guard until you are ready to fire. Draw the pistol from the holster and start the movement that will bring it to your dominant eye. As it comes up, your support hand will meet the dominant hand and wrap around it, forming a good grip.

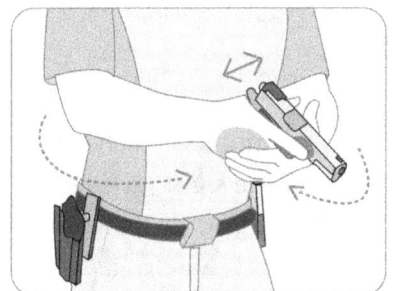 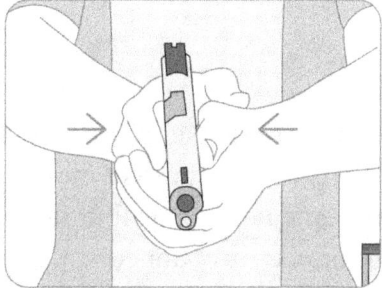

Draw - Position 2

You want your support hand to have as much contact with the pistol's frame as you can. When your support hand is in position under the trigger guard, clamp it tightly, and continue the movement to Position 3.

Position 3

With both hands positioned correctly on your gun, your pistol should be fully presented at eye level with the sight picture on the target.

Draw - Position 3

Some people like to use a "press-out" technique, which follows an arc, but most prefer moving straight to the sight picture. Both movements are fine, but keep in mind that you do not want to introduce any unnecessary movement that would take time away from getting your sights on target.

Checks

Semi-Auto: Check the rotation of your support hand's wrist. You want your thumb pointed at the target and touching the side of the frame. Watch your support hand's thumb; you don't want it to touch the reciprocating slide in any way.

Revolver: Check that your fingers are *not* near the front of or touching the cylinder. Hot gasses and high pressures are released as you fire each shot, and they can burn or damage fingers.

Remember to stay focused on the target as the gun is presented, and make sure you do not place your finger inside the trigger guard until you are ready to fire.

Video

It's a good idea to record a video of yourself to see how smoothly you move through each step. You want to be as efficient as possible, eliminating any unnecessary movements that do not contribute to solid performance. It is a good idea to practice this sequence slowly using each position. Try it first in dry-fire, ensuring you have proper technique, then work on speed after you are consistent with each step.

Other Starting Positions

There are other starting positions you may see in USPSA competition. These include starting with your hands on a wall or starting with your hands on a table.

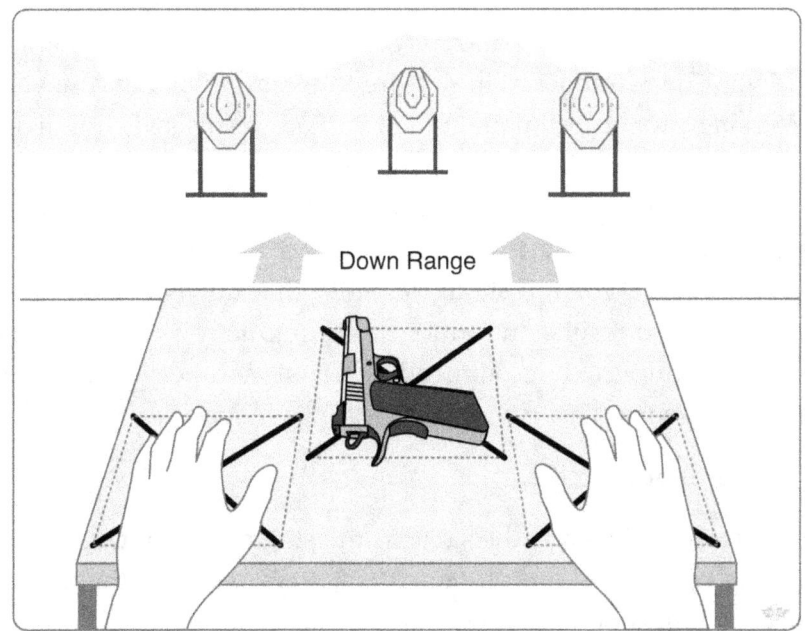

Table Start Example

Anytime you start with the gun in the holster, you will use all three positions to draw the gun. If the gun starts on a table or barrel, use Positions 2 and 3 as you build your grip and present the gun on target.

You will also see starting positions wherein you start facing away from the shooting area and you are required to turn your body and draw. The critical sequence in this case is to turn your body first to face downrange, then draw. You want to be sure that you don't draw your gun before facing downrange, as this will get you disqualified for unsafe gun handling.

Testing your draw technique

Live-fire is the best way to test your skills after you have practiced in dry-fire. Do this at a range where you can wear your holster and safely practice drawing, gripping, and firing several shots at speed.

Single-Shot Exercise

Set up a cardboard or paper target at five to seven yards. Practice your draw sequence in dry-fire to warm up and ensure you are using proper technique. When you are ready, switch to live-fire. Start by drawing and placing one shot on your target. You are testing your ability to draw, build your grip, get a sight picture, execute good trigger control, and place one shot where you want it to go. You should practice this slowly, focusing on technique and results. Introduce speed gradually as your performance improves. I recommend you use a timer with a par feature when you are ready to measure your speed.

Double-Shot Exercise

The second drill starts the same as the single shot on target, but instead of firing one shot, you will fire two shots at the target, placing both shots as close together as possible. Start the drill the same way, using the same technique you followed in the single-shot exercise. As you fire your first shot, keep watching your sights so you are aware of how they are tracking. As the sights return to the target after the first shot's recoil, you should see them return to the same place. When you see them line up again, prep the trigger and take the second shot, placing it as close as possible to the first one. Take your time, as this is not a speed test. It is about seeing your sights lift in recoil and return to the same place. You can gradually increase your speed on any drill, but always stay focused on executing a good technique.

Self-Check

- Does your technique support getting multiple shots close together quickly?
- Do you see the sights lift and return to the same place after recoil?
- Is your trigger control consistent, so you are not introducing movement on the gun to one side or otherwise away from your original point of aim?
- Are you anticipating the shot and flinching, introducing movement away from where you aimed initially?

If any of the above applies, do not worry—this is a normal response when you start. However, be aware of these pitfalls, take it slow, and build proper technique for good results. The closer and tighter the shot groups are at speed, the better. You can adjust the distance to the targets for more insight into your performance, but don't expect your times to be as fast at longer distances. It is recommended that you take the time to see your sights and execute a proper technique, as flaws in your skills will be more visible at longer distances.

RELOADING

In USPSA competitions, you will need more rounds than a single magazine will hold when shooting longer stages. The SCSA Steel Challenge, however, does not incorporate any mandatory reloading as part of your stage performance in competition. Reloading is an important fundamental component when competing in USPSA. Knowing how and when to do it will significantly improve your score. Learning to reload on the move is one of the best uses of time when moving from one shooting location to another.

Essential points:

- Keep your finger off the trigger and outside the trigger guard until you are back up on target and ready to fire.
- Hit the pistol's magazine release to drop the magazine in the pistol and use your support hand to grasp a fresh magazine from your belt at the same time.
- Angle the pistol's magazine well at your belt as you bring the fresh magazine up to reload.
- Hold the magazine in your palm and place your index finger on the front side of the magazine to confirm the bullets are facing the right direction.
- Focus on the magazine well as you insert and firmly seat the fresh magazine using your palm.
- Shift your eyes to the target and reestablish your support hand's grip as you bring the pistol up ready to fire.

One of the best ways to practice and improve your reloading technique is through dry-fire drills. Ensure that your gun and all magazines are unloaded. When you practice, focus on technique, not speed. As you improve your technique, speed will naturally improve with it. Begin by inserting an empty magazine into the pistol and extend your arms using the proper grip and sight picture. You should aim at a target and simulate the same movements needed when executing a reload in competition.

Keep your trigger finger completely off the trigger, out of the trigger guard, and pointed in the same direction as the barrel. Always practice and perform reloads with your finger off the trigger and outside the trigger guard. The easiest way to be consistent is to place your index finger above the trigger guard, touching the slide.

Bring the gun back toward your eyes, high enough so you can watch the entire reloading process easily. You may hear this position referred to as your "workspace."

Drop the magazine from the gun by firmly pressing the magazine release with your dominant hand's thumb. You may need to change your grip and rotate slightly to hit the magazine-release button with the required pressure to drop the magazine.

Keep your eyes on the magazine well and let the ejected magazine fall to the ground. It is a good idea to point the pistol's magazine well at your belt, or the place where your fresh magazine will be coming from. This will make loading the magazine faster and easier.

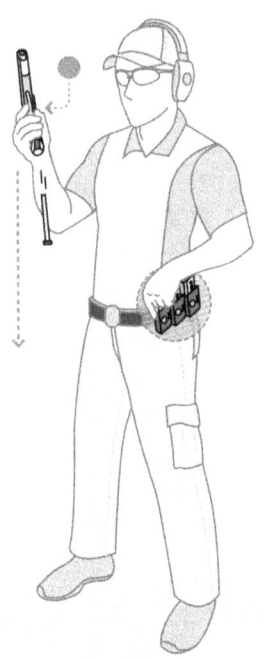
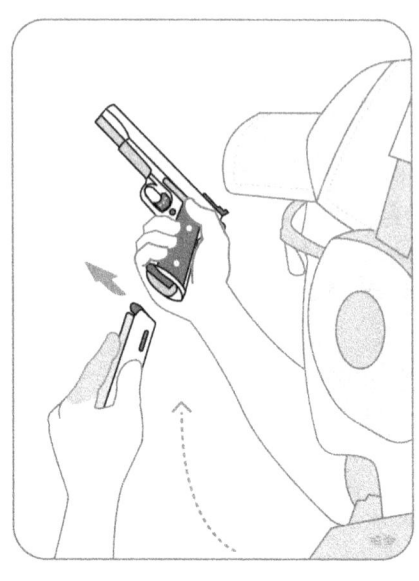

At the same time as you are releasing the magazine, your support hand should be reaching for a magazine off your belt. Use your index finger to ensure the bullets are facing the direction needed to reload before you insert them into the magazine well.

Keep your eyes on the pistol in front of you and focus on where you want the magazine to go. Look directly at the magazine well as you insert the magazine with your support hand, using the palm of your hand to drive it into place.

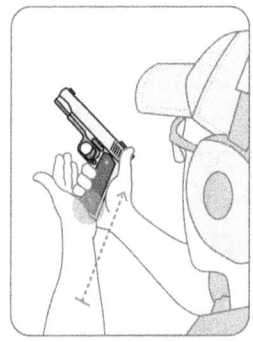 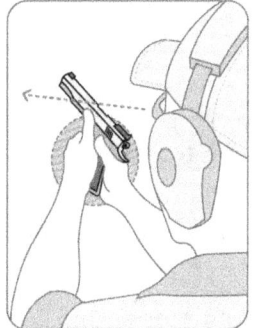 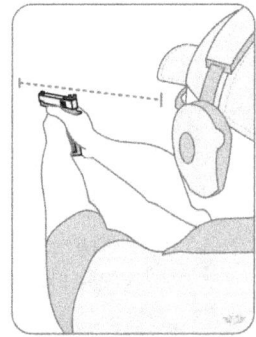

Continue the motion to reengage with your support hand as you present the gun back on target. Practice your skills slowly and deliberately, focusing on proper technique.

Live-Fire

When you are ready to practice in live-fire, follow the same process outlined above. Practice firing to slide lock and reloading, or execute a reload before the gun goes empty. Both methods will simulate what will happen in competition.

Testing your reloading technique

Start by loading all your magazines with two rounds each and place them on your belt. To practice shooting to side lock, load and shoot two shots, execute a reload, and repeat. Practice a sequence of reloads using all your magazines, reloading from a different location on your belt.

To practice shooting before a slide lock, fire one shot and perform a reload and repeat. You can mix both types of practice by alternating between a slide lock reload or gun-loaded reload. Remember to keep your finger out of the trigger guard and off the trigger at all times during the reloading process.

SUMMARY

- You want to ensure good technique on your draw and be able to look at a target and have your gun follow.
- Practice starting positions like "wrists below belt," "wrists above shoulders," and table starts in dry-fire to build your skills.
- Practice using a shot timer with a par-time feature to measure your overall skill performance.
- Video yourself and review your skills as you execute draws and reloads.
- Practice in dry-fire and test yourself in live-fire.
- Practice proper technique in dry-fire and then confirm your skill results in live-fire.

CHAPTER 23
DRY-FIRING

Dry-Fire

Dry-fire is the practice of firearm manipulation without any ammunition. The focus is on building your competency and core skills using the same equipment you would use in live-fire or competition.

The big difference: **THERE IS NEVER ANY AMMUNITION PRESENT WHEN YOU DRY-FIRE. EVER!**

Dry-fire is a simple way to get focused on your fundamental firearm-handling skills and is one of the most inexpensive, highest value activities you can do to become a more proficient competitor. Dry-fire allows you to practice all aspects of shooting and firearm manipulation except recoil control. If you practice proper technique at least ten minutes a day over a few weeks, you *will* see positive results the next time you go to the range.

Dry-Fire Safety

The fact that it is so simple to practice at home makes it convenient, but you must ensure you follow *all* the rules of firearm safety. Check that your firearm is unloaded and cannot become loaded with live ammunition as you practice. Be sure to create a safe working environment and practice conditions before you start. Do not allow yourself to be interrupted or distracted. Safety comes first.

Never have any ammunition nearby or in the same area when working with your firearm or practicing dry-fire. Always take the necessary precautions to ensure a safe practice area. If you have a basement, this can provide additional safety due to the thicker walls that may stop an accidental discharge. Always keep the gun pointed in a safe direction and follow all the rules of firearm safety while practicing.

Benefits

Practice through dry-fire gives all firearm owners a way to develop competency. It's a great way to get acquainted with your firearm features and their operation, as practice builds knowledge and confidence in your abilities. You will also notice that you are more consistent during live-fire, as you will be using the proper techniques for grip, sight picture, and trigger control.

Targets

You will need a few simple targets that resemble what you encounter in a competition. It helps to use smaller targets when you need to simulate distance. For example, a full-size target at ten yards could be simulated with a half-size target at five yards or a quarter-size target at two and a half yards. Proportional targets give you more options to work with as you create your practice area. Practicing at different distances develops the right skills for what you will encounter in competition.

Timer

You will need a shooting timer, specifically one that has a par-time feature. After you construct your dry-fire drill, you can set different par times to test your skill and work on improving efficiency. Par times are a great way to set goals and measure performance improvements. Be sure you are focused on building proper techniques and check your par-time skills at the range using live-fire.

Skills and Goals

It is good to start any dry-fire session with a plan on what you are going to work on and how you will measure success. The following are some fundamental pistol manipulation skills anyone can start with:

- Pulling the trigger without disturbing the sights on a target.
- Building the proper grip and presentation from a holster.
- Drawing to a target and executing proper trigger control.
- Reloading and getting back up on target.
- Clearing malfunctions and getting the sights back on target.
- Practicing dominant-hand and support-hand grip and trigger control.

By practicing more often and focusing on proper technique, your skills will improve quickly with each dry-fire session.

SUMMARY

- Never have any ammunition present when you dry-fire. *Ever*!
- Dry-fire is the least expensive, highest value activity you can do to improve your skills.
- Get some simple targets that resemble what you will be seeing in competition. Use scaled-down versions to help simulate distance.
- Use a timer with a par-time feature and random start to help you measure time and improve responsiveness.
- Watch your sights as you pull the trigger to ensure you are using good technique, and confirm your skills using live-fire at the range.

For additional material on dry-firing, see the companion website at https://pistolshootingsports.com/book-bonus.

CHAPTER 24
MEASURING TIME

Shot timers are essential to measure performance at speed. A timer can be of assistance during dry-fire or live-fire practice sessions. The shot timer will provide details around the speed of your draw, transition times between targets, and the timing of follow-up shots. When you log your times, you can evaluate your performance and determine where to fine-tune.

Measures and Methods

- **Time to first shot** - The duration measured from a start signal to the first shot on target. Useful for gauging draw speed performance.
- **Split times or splits** - The duration between shots on the same target. Useful for measuring a competitor's ability to control recoil and perform follow-up shots on the same target.
- **Transitions** - The duration between shots on different targets. Useful for measuring efficiency as you move to a new target or position.

- **Total elapsed time** - The duration of time from a start signal to the final shot. Ideal for gauging overall stage times and general drill performance.
- **Par times** - A standard measure of performance that uses pre-established start/stop intervals for completing various skills and drills on the clock.
- **Start signal** - The timer can be configured to signal your start in various ways, and the signal can be triggered instantly—after a countdown period or randomly. Using a random start feature will help you develop better reaction times.

As you practice, your speed will improve, and the feedback the timer provides will demonstrate how you're progressing.

Time to First Shot

Time to first shot is a great way to assess your draw performance. However, you must ensure that you are building your grip, obtaining a good sight picture, and placing the shot where you intend. Establish your baseline and refrain from throwing the gun up and just pulling the trigger in less than a second. Use proper techniques so you do not need to relearn the fundamentals later.

When you are comfortable with your technique, look at areas where you can make incremental improvements to reduce your performance time. Establish a par time of 1.8 seconds initially to finish the draw, find your target, and accurately place the first shot. Once you are comfortable reaching the initial par time, incrementally reduce it by one-tenth of a second until you find your current optimal performance.

Quantifying Multiple Performances

Averages are beneficial in assessing multiple performance scores and times, as it is helpful to be aware of your average skill times for draws and multiple shots on targets at different distances. Track your personal bests so you know what your capabilities are. Review your averages to see where your consistency is improving. As your average improves, so will your consistency.

Split Times or Splits

Splits measure the duration between shots on the same target. This measure helps you see the length of time needed to recover from the first shot's recoil and place reliable follow-up shots on the same target.

Split measures are useful because they tell you the cost in time to recover from recoil to place a follow-up shot. As you work this skill, ensure you are following proper technique to get the right baseline.

For example, set up three targets: T1 at ten yards, T2 at twenty yards, and T3 at thirty yards. Engage all three targets at the start signal, taking whatever time is needed to place a pair of shots on each target using proper technique. Refer to the diagram below.

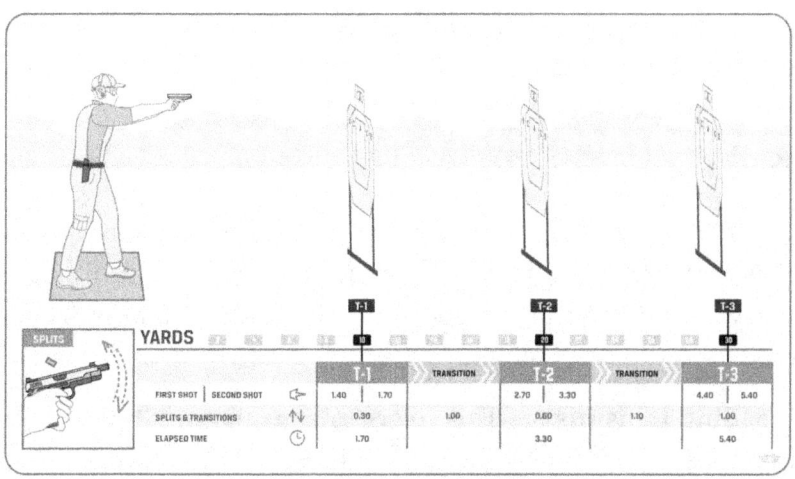

Splits and Transitions

When you are shooting two shots on the same target from a close distance, you will achieve quicker shot-to-shot splits. As you move farther away, your split times will become slower. It takes longer to confirm a good sight picture and place a scoring shot on targets at a distance.

Let's say the first shot on T1 was 1.4 seconds and the follow-up shot on T1 was recorded at 1.7 seconds. That gives you a 0.3-second split time between shots on the first target.

As you transition to the T2 target, you add 1.0 second of transition time. Your first shot on T2 was at 2.7 seconds and the second shot on T2 was at 3.3 seconds. That gives you a 0.6-second split time between shots at twenty yards.

As you transition to the T3 target, you take 1.1 seconds of transition time. Your first shot on T3 was at 4.4 seconds and the second shot on T3 was at 5.4 seconds. That gives you a 1.0 split time between shots at thirty yards and a total time of 5.4 seconds.

Understanding the amount of time needed at different distances will help you understand what is needed to achieve competitive scoring shots—rather than just firing a couple of shots and hoping for the best.

Transitions

Transitions measure the time between shots on different targets. This measure is helpful to determine efficiency when shifting to a new target or location. There are two fundamental transition types: standing and moving.

Standing transitions - This refers to engaging multiple targets from the same shooting location. These don't measure movement, only your ability to acquire the next target.

Moving transitions - This looks at how efficiently you can transition to a different shooting location and engage a target. Assessing transition movement reveals where time is spent moving on a stage and which movements have the highest time cost. Whenever you are moving locations, take the quickest route to reduce your overall stage time. When competing on larger stages in USPSA, transition times become a significant contributor to your overall score. Knowing where you need to accelerate and improve transition time is essential to achieving a high score.

Total Elapsed Time

The total elapsed time is the duration of time from the start signal to a final shot. It is beneficial for gauging drills and overall stage performance. As you measure more parts of your performance, you will see areas where you can shave off time. This will contribute to faster stage times and improved scores. When you break down the details of each activity, you can better understand the time cost of those activities on stage.

Par Time

Par times are a great way to practice gun manipulations in live-fire or dry-fire situations. The feature helps quantify the performance of completing skills on the clock using a preset start and stop signal.

Par-time drills are ideal for dry-fire practice because the sound markers signal the beginning and end of each exercise. When you have mastered a par-time drill in dry-fire, test your performance in live-fire. You don't want to create a situation where things look good in dry-fire but don't work when you get on the range. Be sure you are building on proper techniques, and always check your par time performance using live-fire.

. . .

Start Signals

Timers can be configured to signal your start in multiple ways.

- **Instant** - The timer starts as soon as the start button is triggered. Instant start works great when you have a partner that can run you on a stage or drill.
- **Countdown** - The timer starts after a specific number of seconds from the start button being triggered. This is convenient when you are by yourself practicing drills.
- **Random** - The timer will choose a random delay after the start button is triggered. This is a great way to work by yourself to develop reaction time. The random start is supported by many timers and helps you to not "game" starts by simulating an actual person.

SUMMARY

- When you are comfortable with your technique, start using a timer to measure your speed. Timers are great tools to help evaluate speed and performance and will help you find places to improve.
- It is important to understand the different measures and methods used in shot timers so you can evaluate your performance in practice sessions.
- Track your par-time performance as you challenge yourself with tighter par times and various assessments. You'll quickly notice the improvements in your skill level and confidence.

CHAPTER 25
MALFUNCTIONS AND CLEARING

You will have malfunctions from time to time in practice (and hopefully, fewer times in a match). Recognizing the type of failure and executing the right recovery technique is the best way to get back in the game.

In competition, you want to focus on your best performance and not have to troubleshoot or fix problems. Work through any suspected issues in your practice sessions and take notes on the frequency, causes, and how you remedied the failure. Your notes will help you see the frequency of an issue and any contributing factors. Routine maintenance, cleaning, and lubrication can go a long way in ensuring good operation and a solid understanding of how your firearm operates.

Safety

The first thing to remember as you start working to clear malfunctions is keeping the firearm pointed in a safe direction at all times. Ensure you keep your finger out of the trigger guard and off the trigger. You don't want to accidentally fire a round while you are working to fix a problem. Eject your magazine, make the gun safe, and show clear before you start correcting a malfunction. Always ensure safety first, before you begin troubleshooting.

Malfunctions and Clearing

For competitive pistol shooting, you are not in a life-or-death situation, and you will want to spend more time reviewing and diagnosing a malfunction's cause and effect. Take the time to look closely at the type of malfunction you are experiencing so you can take proper action.

The three most common types of malfunctions:

1. Failure to Feed

After shooting a round, the gun does not cycle correctly and fails to load the next round in the chamber. Check to see that the magazine is fully inserted, then rack the slide fully to the rear and let it go. If you continue to have a problem, eject the magazine, rotate the pistol so all rounds will fall as you pull the slide to the rear and hold it open. Rotate the gun back so you can see into the open ejection port. Check that all rounds are removed from the pistol. Insert a fresh magazine, fully rack the slide, and check that the pistol loaded correctly.

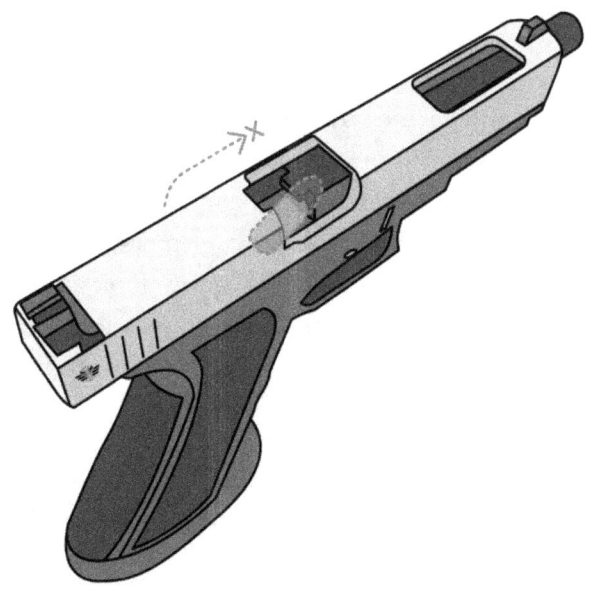

Failure to Feed

Sometimes the magazine is not seated correctly, or you may have a magazine that is overloaded; therefore, the spring does not have enough tension to push the bullet to the top of the magazine's feed lips. Keeping your magazines clean and adjusted will help them feed more efficiently. If the springs wear down, you should replace or adjust them.

You may not be holding the firearm securely. If you aren't, the force needed to cycle the gun will not be transmitted to the slide. A poor grip causes the pistol to rock in your hands, so ensure you are not introducing this issue as the gun fires and cycles.

2. Failure to Fire

You loaded a round and pulled the trigger, but nothing happened. When you troubleshoot, keep the firearm pointed in a safe direction and your finger off the trigger. Eject the magazine, then clear the round, paying close attention to its condition. Note: If the bullet is *not* in the cartridge, you may have an unsafe condition, see Unsafe Conditions and do not fire the gun.

If the bullet is still in the cartridge, you may not have enough force from the firing pin or hammer to detonate the primer and cause the gun to fire correctly. This condition is referred to as a "light strike" and can be caused by primers not being seated properly or weak springs. Take a good look at the bullet's primer to see if there is a mark or dimple in the primer. Is the dimple in the center? Is it shallower, when compared to a cartridge that worked?

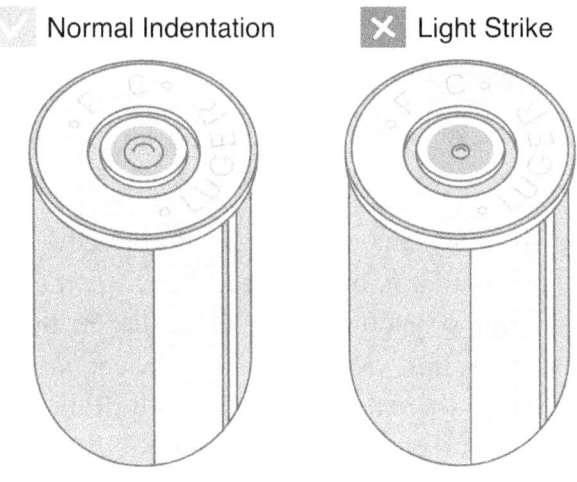

Did anything change recently with ammunition, magazines, springs, cleaning, or lubrication? Make a record of what you observe around any failure. If the problem continues, try cleaning and lubricating your gun. You may need to replace any worn-out springs. Have the firearm inspected or repaired by an authorized gunsmith to ensure proper operation and safety.

• • •

3. Failure to Eject

This is where the gun fires, but the case does not eject all the way and gets stuck in the gun's slide, preventing the pistol from fully cycling. This condition is easy to spot because the round fired okay, but the empty case is held in the ejection port. Rotate the pistol so the spent cartridge will fall as you pull the slide to the rear and hold it open. Rotate the gun back so you can see into the open ejection port. Release the slide and check that the pistol is loaded correctly. If you continue to have a problem, eject the magazine, fully rack the slide until all rounds are removed, and insert a fresh magazine.

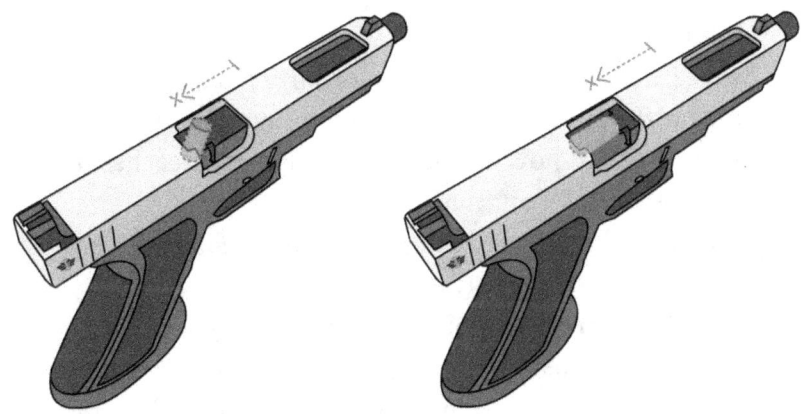

Failure to Eject

Check your springs to see if they are too strong or too tight to permit your selected rounds to fire and cycle. Your gun may need cartridge loads that create more pressure to fully cycle correctly. Check to see if you have a weak or broken extractor that does not apply the proper pressure or action to eject the spent cartridge fully.

• • •

Troubleshooting Checklist

- **Cleaning**: When was the last time you cleaned and lubricated your firearm? Carbon can build up after lots of rounds and training sessions. Some ammunition will increase the carbon buildup faster than others.
- **Recoil Springs**: Does your pistol move easily into battery with a round in the chamber? You may have worn out the recoil springs. This can cause the slide to not cycle with enough force to properly seat the cartridge and place the gun in battery. Springs that are too strong for your bullet loads may prevent the gun from fully cycling. Using the right springs for your ammunition will help ensure consistent operation.
- **Magazines**: Do you have worn or dirty magazines? Some pistols are very picky about spring pressures from magazines and how the bullet is angled as it reaches the feed lips. Check your magazines for weak or dirty springs, and whether the tops of your magazine's feed lips are shaped correctly.
- **Cartridges**: Are the primers on the cartridges seated correctly? If you are shooting reloads, make sure the primer is fully pressed into the cartridge base. Does the cartridge move smoothly into the barrel chamber? Check the length of cartridges and the shape of the brass for defects.
- **Gun Handling**: Check that you are not introducing a malfunction by touching the slide and reducing its operation as it cycles from shot to shot. Check that you are holding the gun firmly so the recoil causes the gun to cycle as designed.

SUMMARY

- As you are working to clear a malfunction, always keep your finger out of the trigger guard and keep the firearm pointed in a safe direction at all times.
- Safety is the most important thing to remember as you work to clear a malfunction.
- Remove all ammunition before you begin troubleshooting.
- Review the different types of malfunctions and understand how to clear them effectively.
- Review the troubleshooting checklist for things that contribute to the most common malfunctions.

CHAPTER 26
UNSAFE CONDITIONS

Unsafe Conditions

If at any time you suspect or experience an unsafe condition with your firearm, keep the gun pointed in a safe direction, remove all ammunition, and get the firearm inspected or repaired by an authorized gunsmith.

Slam Fire

Slam fire is when there is an unintended discharge or ignition as you are loading a round in the chamber of the pistol. Ensure you always have your trigger finger off the trigger and outside the trigger guard as you chamber a round. Keep the pistol pointed downrange in a safe direction whenever you chamber a round. If you experience an unintended discharge of any kind wherein you did not touch the trigger, you should have your pistol checked by a certified gunsmith and repaired before using it again.

Squibs

A squib is a very serious condition where a bullet gets stuck in the barrel of the gun. You *never* want to fire a "round" when you have a plugged barrel, as the extra pressure buildup is very dangerous. When pressure can't be released as designed, the pressure can destroy the gun in your hand and cause injury. Take care if you think you have this condition, and ensure the firearm is unloaded and safe before any inspection.

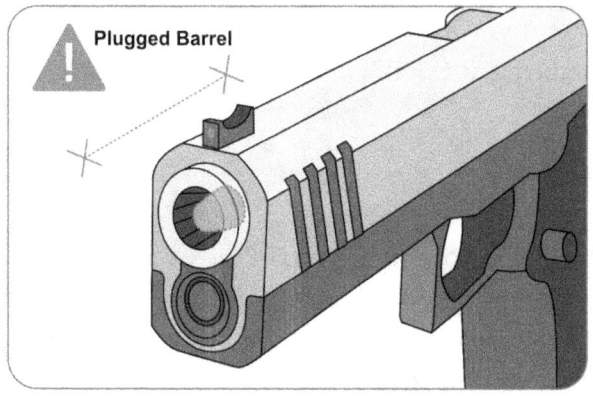

Squib

Squibs are usually caused by one round that did not receive the correct powder charge when it was loaded. You may hear the primer go off, but the firearm does not cycle. A light powder load does not create enough pressure to push the bullet all the way through the barrel and cycle the gun. Squibs can happen when new reloaders have not learned to check each cartridge as it gets charged with powder.

Any time you have a plugged barrel, it creates an unsafe condition that needs to be corrected before you use your firearm. You can't clear a squib without tools, and you should seek out an authorized gunsmith to return your firearm to a safe working condition. An experienced gunsmith will have specific tools to remove the stuck bullet without scratching the inside of the barrel or damaging your firearm.

• • •

Hang Fire

A hang fire is when a round has a delayed discharge. You press the trigger, the firing pin or hammer strikes the cartridge, but there is an unexpected delay in the ignition of the round. Take your time and always keep the gun pointed downrange in a safe direction as you work through this kind of issue. Check your ammunition if you experience a hang fire; the ammo may be old or damaged, and you will want to dispose of it safely.

SUMMARY

- Always keep your finger out of the trigger guard and keep the firearm pointed in a safe direction at all times.
- Safety is the most important thing to remember as you work on your firearm.
- Remove all ammunition before you begin troubleshooting.
- Review the different types of unsafe conditions and recognize how to identify them.
- An unsafe condition can be caused by a firearm that is not in safe working order. Have the firearm inspected or repaired by an authorized gunsmith to ensure proper operation and safety.

PART V
ON THE RANGE

CHAPTER 27
COLD RANGE, STORAGE, AND CARRY

COLD RANGE

All USPSA and SCSA events are held on what is known as a cold range. This means you cannot bring a loaded firearm onto the range. This also includes concealed-carry guns. If you are in law enforcement, check with the match organizers before you arrive so they can provide you with a place to *safely* unload.

It is imperative that you arrive at the range with an unloaded firearm in a secure bag or case.

STORAGE AND CARRY

All firearms must be kept unloaded until a competitor is operating under the direction of a range officer (RO). It's not until the range officer instructs competitors to "load and make ready" from a designated shooting box that they can safely engage in competition.

If you bring a loaded gun to a match without being under the direction of a certified range officer, you will be disqualified.

Competitors should arrive at the range with their unloaded firearm in a secure case or bag. The secure container must completely cover the gun and prevent access to the trigger. Many competitors use specialized padded bags that zip closed, preventing access to the firearm.

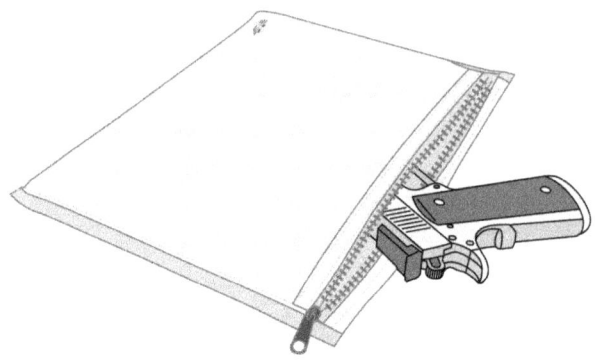

Zippered Pistol Storage Sleeve

Steel Challenge (SCSA) competitors shooting rimfire and USPSA PCC competitors shooting rifles do not use holsters and may transport their unloaded firearms between stages in secure cases or bags.

Unloaded center-fire pistols should be placed in a safe and secure holster, attached to a belt on their person, from inside the safety area. Do not remove your holster with a gun in it. Go to the safety area and place the unloaded firearm in a secure case or bag before removing your holster. When you are carrying a handgun holstered, you must have an empty magazine well and the hammer or striker must be fully de-cocked.

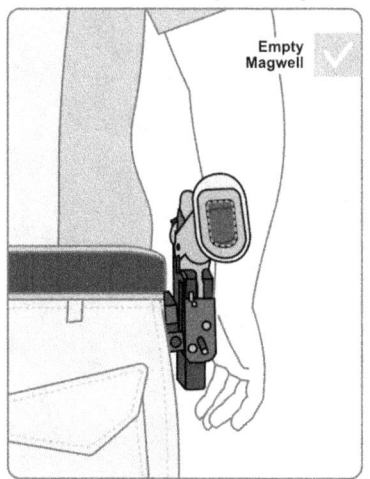
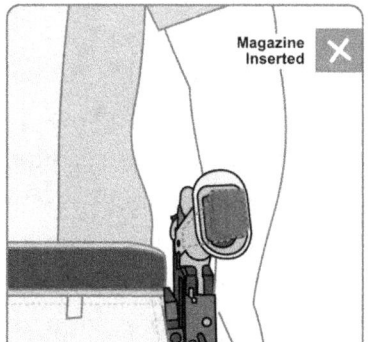

Under no circumstances is a competitor permitted to leave a course of fire in possession of a loaded firearm. Failure to follow SCSA and USPSA rules for transporting, carrying, and storage will result in disqualification.

Some firearm competitions are designed to support multiple firearms and equipment types on a single stage. USPSA and SCSA competitions are designed around one firearm per match division entry. Competitors must never use or wear more than one firearm during a single course of fire. Division competitors must use the same firearm type and sights for all stages and courses of fire in a match. The rules do not allow significant modifications to a firearm during a match without the approval of the range master.

Some SCSA and USPSA matches may allow competitors to register for multiple divisions in the same match. If you are allowed to shoot multiple divisions, you still need to use the same firearm for each division it is registered under.

SUMMARY

- All USPSA and SCSA events are held on cold ranges. You cannot bring a loaded firearm onto the range, and this includes concealed-carry guns.
- All firearms should be transported unloaded in a secure bag or case.
- Secure storage containers should cover the firearm completely, preventing access to the trigger.

CHAPTER 28
SAFETY AREAS

Safety areas are designated places where you are allowed to take your firearm out of its carry case and manipulate it in a safe, consistent direction. You must always keep the gun pointed into the berm or designated safe direction when you are within the safety area.

Safety areas are the only designated areas where you are allowed to handle your gun when you are not actively shooting under the direction of a range officer. These areas will be clearly identified by signs. Safety areas include a table and a safe direction for you to keep the firearm pointed.

Safety Area

Do not handle any ammunition in the safety area! You may enter the safety area with loaded magazines on your belt, but you may not touch or handle them at any time. This also applies to simulated rounds and dummy ammunition.

You can load magazines and handle ammunition anywhere *except* the safety area. Remember, the only time you may load your firearm with ammunition during a match is under the direction of a range officer in a designated shooting area. Never handle any rounds in the safety area under any circumstances.

Things you can do in the safety area while facing the designated safe direction with an unloaded firearm:

- Handle unloaded firearms and accessories.
- Take your unloaded gun in and out of a secure case.
- Holster and unholster.

- Practice drawing and dry-firing.
- Handle empty magazines, inserting and ejecting them from the gun.
- Cycling, inspection, maintenance, repair, and cleaning of your firearm.

It is essential that you do not overcrowd the area, as this could create an unsafe condition. Wait outside the designated area until it is safe to enter. After you have tested your unloaded firearm, you must place it back into your secure case or holster *before* leaving the safety area.

SUMMARY

- Safety areas are designated locations where you may remove a firearm from its case or holster and manipulate it in the designated safe direction.
- No ammunition of any kind may be handled inside the safety area. This includes live and dummy rounds.
- Do not overcrowd the safety area or create an unsafe condition.

CHAPTER 29
180 RULE AND SAFE ANGLES

180 RULE

The 180 rule focuses on where the muzzle of your gun is pointing. In shooting sports, the terms "downrange" and "up-range" are used to describe designated (downrange) and unsafe (up-range) shooting directions. Downrange is the 180 degrees of safe shooting direction. Up-range is the unsafe 180 degrees of shooting direction, away from the targets.

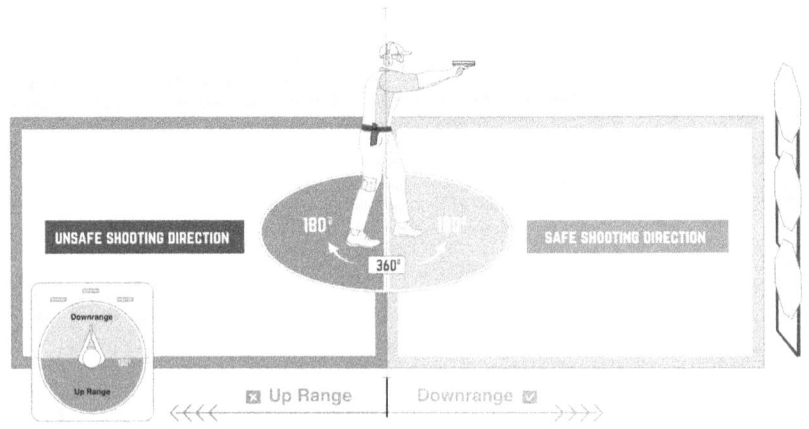

180 Rule - Safe Shooting Direction

Before you start any stage, it is important to understand the 180-degree plane and how it moves with you as you engage the course of fire.

Breaking the 180 rule can happen when competitors are on the move and are not aware of the direction they are facing. Sometimes this can happen when a competitor brings a gun up to reload and is not aware of where it is pointing. (See the right-handed example below.)

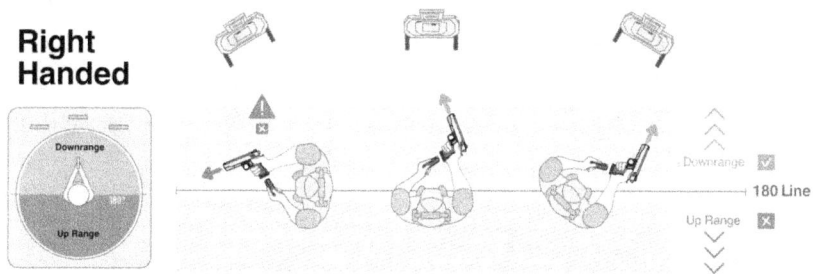

Right Handed Competitor - Reloading

Right-handed competitors need to watch where the gun is pointing as they reload when their right side is facing downrange.

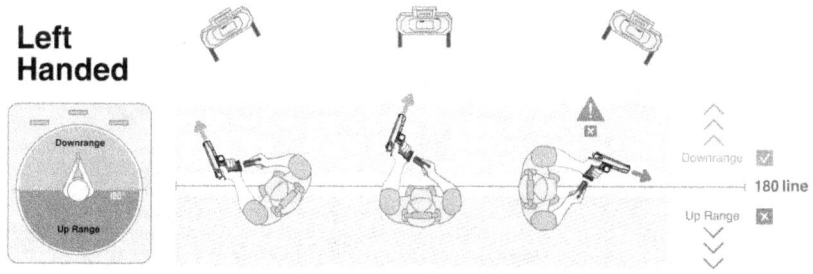

Left Handed Competitor - Reloading

Left-handed competitors need to watch where the gun is pointing when their left side is facing downrange.

Be mindful as you move on a stage from location to location, or when clearing a malfunction, that your gun is purposefully pointing downrange. Failure to follow the 180 rule will result in a competitor's disqualification from the match.

SAFE ANGLES

Course designs must always ensure safe angles of fire so USPSA and SCSA course designers must consider ricochets, backstops, berms, and target placements when constructing a stage to provide participants and spectators safe and reliable course designs. Always review the written stage brief so you understand how a stage is designed to work and you do not violate the 180 rule or safe angles of fire.

SUMMARY

- The 180 rule focuses on where the muzzle of your firearm is pointing.
- Review and understand the differences between downrange and up-range and how the 180 plane follows the competitor as they engage the course of fire.
- Review stage design and safe angles of fire before you compete on them. Have a stage plan that includes safe reloading positions so you do not risk breaking the 180 rule.

CHAPTER 30
FINGER OFF THE TRIGGER AND SWEEPING

FINGER OFF THE TRIGGER

It is highly recommended that you get into the habit of having your finger outside the trigger guard and off the trigger's face until your firearm is up and on target.

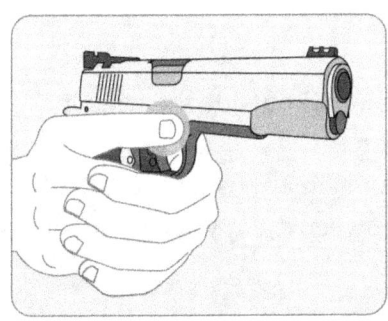 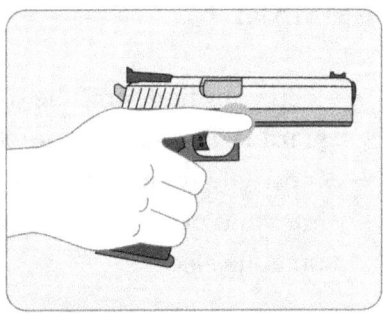

Keeping your finger straight down the side helps the range officer see you are following this rule and ensures you have good form. You don't want to be moving or manipulating your firearm and accidentally fire off a round. This is called an "accidental discharge" (or AD) and causes a bullet to go somewhere you did not intend. This is the quickest way to draw everyone's attention toward unsafe gun handling skills, so keep your finger off the trigger until you are aiming at a target.

Failure to follow safe gun handling rules will result in a competitor's disqualification from the match.

SWEEPING

Sweeping is when the muzzle of your firearm points at any part of your body or someone else's as you move about a stage. Anytime you are moving with a firearm, know where the muzzle is pointing at all times.

Avoid sweeping your support hand, arms, and legs as you reload, move, or manipulate stage props. Sweeping can happen as you focus on other activities besides safe gun handling.

Failure to follow safe gun handling rules will result in a competitor's disqualification from the match.

SUMMARY

- Keep your finger off the trigger and outside the trigger guard until you are ready to fire.
- Know where the muzzle of your firearm is pointed at all times and ensure you are not sweeping at yourself or someone else.

CHAPTER 31
SPORTSMANSHIP AND PROHIBITED SUBSTANCES

SPORTSMANSHIP

You may be disqualified if a range officer believes you have conducted yourself in an unsportsmanlike manner. This can include behavior that violates the official rules, negatively impacts other competitors, or creates an unfair condition. Be sure to review the official rules and comply with match officials' directions during competition.

Refer to Section 8.4 of the SCSA competition rules for more detail: https://scsa.org/rules.

Refer to Section 10.6 of the USPSA competition rules for more detail: https://uspsa.org/rules.

Unsportsmanlike conduct detracts from the sport and the individual. Bring your best attitude to the range, as everyone is there to enjoy the sport, be safe, and have fun.

PROHIBITED SUBSTANCES

All shooting sports require participants to be in complete control and are responsible for their actions at all times, both physically and mentally. There is no tolerance for the use of nonprescription drugs or alcohol. Competitors may not be under the influence or affected by alcohol or drugs of any kind during competition.

Refer to Section 8.3 of the SCSA rules for more detail:

https://scsa.org/rules.

Refer to Section 10.7 of the USPSA rules for more detail:

https://uspsa.org/rules.

SUMMARY

- Be safe, smart, sober, and in control at all times.

CHAPTER 32
SAFETY VIOLATIONS AND DISQUALIFICATION

You are expected to understand how to be safe and how to keep everyone else safe by following competition and range-specific rules at all times. This includes ensuring control of your firearm at all times as you move about the range and compete on stages.

SAFETY VIOLATIONS

When an appointed range officer observes a "safety violation," they will issue the "**STOP**" command. The RO will instruct competitors to ensure their gun and the range is safe before discussing the safety issue. In the case of a dropped gun, the range officer will instruct everyone on how to proceed before the firearm is retrieved safely.

When the range is safe, the match director will usually be called to review the range officer's observation and ensure the competitor understands the violation. The match director will make a decision around disqualification based on the official rules and what the appointed RO observed. It is important to remember that the range officer and match director are there to ensure everyone understands and follows safe rules of competition.

Examples of safety violations include:

Accidental discharge (AD) - The gun goes off without intention, not pointed at an intended target.

Unsafe gun handling - The manipulation of a firearm that causes, or could cause, an unsafe condition. *(Types of unsafe gun handling violations below.)*

- **Handling a firearm outside the designated safety area -** This refers to removing a firearm from a holster or bag outside the safety area, when a range officer has not issued the command to do so.
- **Handling any ammunition inside the safety area -** Any handling of loaded magazines, live or dummy ammunition, when inside the safety area.
- **Unsafe finger placement or riding the trigger** - Resting your finger on the trigger when you are not engaging a target is a quick way to get disqualified. Keep your finger outside the trigger guard until you are ready to fire.
- **Sweeping** - Inadvertently pointing the muzzle of the gun at an arm, leg, body part, or person. Always be aware of where your arms, legs, and the range officers are in relation to where the gun is pointed. Keep the muzzle of the gun out in front of you and pointed in a safe direction.
- **Breaking the 180 rule -** Each course of fire is designed to be engaged safely. Pointing a gun anywhere but downrange is not part of the course of fire. Breaking the 180-degree plane means you have pointed the gun away from the designated shooting area. This can happen when competitors are on the move and not aware of the

direction they are facing. Be mindful as you move from location to location, or when clearing a malfunction, that your gun is purposefully pointing downrange.

DISQUALIFICATIONS

The term "DQ" stands for match disqualification. When a competitor commits a safety violation, they are immediately subject to a match disqualification. Safety violations are taken very seriously. Being awarded a match disqualification helps competitors remember the experience. When a competitor is awarded a match disqualification, they may not shoot or compete for the rest of the competition.

Most pistol shooting competitors have been awarded a match disqualification at least once if they have been competing for a period of time. **The main point of a DQ is to learn from the experience and not repeat the same mistake.**

Know the rules and how to follow them. If you have questions, start with the rule book and then ask a certified range officer or range master. These people have invested time to learn the rules and demonstrate their understanding through certification.

For the full list of rules on safety violations and disqualification, refer to the official SCSA and USPSA rules.

- SCSA Rules: https://scsa.org/rules.
- USPSA Rules: https://uspsa.org/rules.

SUMMARY

Safety is critical at all competitive shooting events and is taken very seriously. Each local range will have specific rules and safety instructions you will want to review and understand.

Things to remember:

- Pointing a firearm in a way that breaks the 180-degree downrange plane will get you disqualified.
- Sweeping or pointing the muzzle of a firearm either at yourself or another person will get you disqualified.
- Placing your finger inside the trigger guard when you are not engaging a target can get you disqualified.
- Ensure safe manipulation and handling of your firearm at all times. This includes while you are in a shooting box and any designated safety areas.
- Handling live ammunition inside the safety area is not permitted; only unloaded firearms may be handled inside the safety area.
- The maximum velocity for any round of ammunition used in USPSA or SCSA is 1,600 feet per second. This limit ensures safety for shooters and spectators wearing proper eye protection at the specified distances.
- All firearms must be kept unloaded until a competitor is operating under the direction of a range officer.
- Listen to the range officer as the stage brief is read. Review the stage, understand the course of fire, and have a stage plan that ensures safe firearm handling skills and movements. Consider where you will be facing for reloads and where you will interact with targets on the stage.
- Dropped firearms. This applies to all firearms, loaded or unloaded. If you ever drop your gun during a match, do not pick it up! Call a range officer to ensure the safe retrieval of the firearm. You do not want to be picking up or handling a gun outside the safe area without a range officer present. Dropping a loaded firearm will get you disqualified and sent home.

CHAPTER 33
RANGE COMMANDS

Range commands are simple and are delivered by the range officer (RO) who is in charge on a given stage. The RO will issue commands to ensure safe and fair completion, and the commands are similar across SCSA Steel Challenge and USPSA shooting sports.

It is imperative that you understand the course of fire so you keep things moving when it is your turn to compete. You should review all written stage briefings to understand the specifics around start position, rules, and round count. Be ready to run the stage before your name is called from shooting order and ensure you have all the necessary magazines loaded.

When it is your turn to compete, wait for the range officer to issue the "make ready" command, as it is crucial that you do not un-bag or unholster your firearm until the RO has told you to do so. The range officer is the official person in charge on a given stage, and you must comply with all their directives.

The following is a list of range commands that you should make yourself familiar with.

Make ready!

This is the first command you will hear. You are under the supervision of the range officer (RO), and they have authorized you to make your firearm ready. By doing so, the RO has verified that the range is clear. Making ready is the signal to handle your firearm in a safe direction. This means it must point downrange at all times. It is best to be deliberate in your actions, so the range officer is aware you understand and are following safety rules and commands.

Note: Part of making ready before you load your firearm is to check your sight picture. You can point the firearm downrange at a target to do this. Checking your sight picture should be done from the start position or no more than one step from that location in USPSA competitions. This is a good habit to get into, and you will see many competitive shooters take the time to compose themselves and see their sights on a target.

When you have completed taking a sight picture, load a magazine and place a round in the chamber. You will need to ensure a safe starting condition for your firearm and safeties so that you comply with your division rules. You will do this in a way that keeps the firearm pointed in a safe direction and allows the RO to see you are following the command.

Firearm Starts

Steel Challenge: Ensure your firearm starts loaded. If you are shooting from a holster, you will place the gun in your holster and will have your wrists above your shoulders just enough so they are visible from behind. If using rifles or rimfire pistols, ensure you have the gun pointed at the "low ready" starting marker with your finger off the trigger.

USPSA: In USPSA, you must follow a specific written brief for each stage. USPSA has many options for firearm starts. For example: gun loaded in holster, gun unloaded on barrel, hands on X's, and so on. The written stage brief will be explicit in its directions for each stage start.

Ready your firearm, facing downrange. Move into the starting position and listen for the next command. If you are not compliant with the starting position—including feet and hands—the RO will let you know. You must acknowledge and comply with the RO's commands to ensure safe and fair competition.

Are you ready?

Everything you have done to prepare for competition has been done. You are about to apply your skill level around speed and accuracy to the stage and have some fun. If you are not ready, it is crucial that you reply to the RO "no" or "not ready." If you are not clear to the range officer that you are not ready, they will assume you are ready and move on to the next command.

Do not waste everyone's time—know what you need to know before you make your way to the shooting box or start position.

Stand by!

"Stand by" should be the last command you hear before the start signal. You are in position and ready to go, so the RO is signaling the transition to the "start signal" or "beep."

Focus and put everything aside except what you are about to do. Many competitors will look at the first target, when it is visible. Within a few seconds, you will hear the start signal to begin your competitive run.

Start signal/beep

Run your stage plan! Be safe, follow the rules, engage the course of fire, and have fun. As you engage targets, you will experience your current level of skill. You may be very good at some skills and not as proficient with others. It is important to stay focused on performing at your level of skill and not react or lose focus from your stage plan. There will be opportunities to review later, but for now, just perform at your current skill level. When you have finished the course of fire safely and successfully delivered your last shot, stop at that location, keep the firearm facing downrange, and await the instructions of the range officer.

Note: In Steel Challenge, you will engage the same course of fire for multiple strings. The RO will instruct you to make ready for each string until you have completed all your runs.

If finished, unload and show clear.

Remove your magazine from the firearm and eject or empty the chamber of any rounds. Your firearm is pointed downrange in a safe direction, your finger is out of the trigger guard, and you are positioned to demonstrate unloading and showing clear to the range officer.

Remove your magazine from the firearm and eject any rounds from the chamber. Lock or hold the slide back in an open position to allow the RO to inspect and verify you are holding an empty gun. (Note: Revolvers are presented with the cylinder out, open, and empty.) You should not have live ammo in your firearm. Wait for the RO to verify and inspect what is needed to ensure safety.

If clear, slide forward, hammer down, and holster.

This command acknowledges that you have demonstrated your firearm is unloaded and clear of ammunition. It is always the competitor's responsibility to ensure the firearm is unloaded and safe.

Keep the firearm pointed downrange as you perform the slide forward and hammer down portion of this command.

Close the slide (slide forward) and release the hammer or firing pin by pulling the trigger. **Always do this pointed downrange, just as you would firing a live round.** The RO is making sure you have an empty gun, and the hammer or firing pin is in a static position. The final command, **"and holster,"** refers to placing your firearm back into your holster securely while facing downrange.

In Steel Challenge, if you are using a rifle or rimfire pistol, you will place them back in your shooting bag or case. If you are shooting a rifle, it is a good idea to use a plastic barrel flag that shows there is nothing in the chamber. The RO may have other things to say that will help you at this point, so listen and comply with their instructions.

Range is clear!

When you have secured your firearm, the RO will say, "Range is clear." This signal advises the squad that you have completed your course of fire and the range is now clear. Your score is recorded, and the course is reset for the next competitor.

Scoring:

Steel Challenge: Scoring is done at the end of each run by recording your time for that string and any penalties. You should review and approve the final recorded score. Larger matches may reset the stage by repainting the steel between each competitor.

USPSA: The scorer and tapers should work together to reset the stage and record your score as efficiently as possible. You will want to stay with the range officer as your targets are reviewed. You should not touch any targets after your run. Follow along, and ensure you understand how your targets are scored. After your stage scoring is complete, you will be asked to review and acknowledge that score on paper or on a digital tablet. You should then collect your ejected magazines lying about the stage so they do not disrupt the next competitor.

Stop!

If you hear this command, stop what you are doing, right where you are. Your finger should be off the trigger and out of the trigger guard, the firearm pointed in a safe direction. If you have a manual safety, you will want to engage it. Listen to the range officer's instruction and follow commands.

If you hear this command, there is always a good reason. A target may have fallen over or not been reset, or there is an unsafe condition on the stage. For example, you could have broken the 180-degree plane, been running with your finger inside the trigger guard, or swept yourself with the muzzle of the firearm. Listen carefully, as the range officer will let you know how they want you to proceed.

Remember, whenever you are loading, reloading, or unloading, your fingers must be outside the trigger guard and the muzzle of the firearm pointed in a safe direction downrange. Again, it is essential to follow your RO's commands to ensure safe and fair competition.

Summary of commands you will hear:

- **Make ready!** - You are the designated competitor at the start position under command of the range officer. The RO has checked to see that the range is clear and reset. It means you can unholster your firearm, take a sight picture, load your firearm, make it safe, holster, and assume the designated start position.
- **Are you ready?** - The RO is ensuring you are ready to go.

- **Stand by!** - The transition time before the start signal (usually a few seconds).
- **Start signal/beep** - You can engage the course of fire.
- **If finished, unload, and show clear** - Unload the magazine, eject the chambered round, and open the slide so the RO can verify your firearm is unloaded.
- **If clear, slide forward, hammer down, and holster** - This command is given after you have verified the empty firearm. Keep the firearm pointed in a safe direction, close the slide, pull the trigger, then holster.
- **Range is clear!** - This is a signal to all squad members that it is now safe to move downrange to score and reset.

PART VI
SCSA COMPETITION

STEEL CHALLENGE SHOOTING ASSOCIATION

CHAPTER 34
HISTORY AND GAME OVERVIEW

Steel Challenge competition shooting is a great way to get started in the pistol shooting sports. It's an excellent place for beginners because the rules and targets are simple, and movement is not a significant factor.

HISTORY

"We founded the Steel Challenge out of our love for the shooting sports. We wanted a match that was challenging and fun but would also be easily understood by non-shooters who would see the competition and find within themselves a greater desire to join the shooting sports." - Mike Fichman. (USPSA "USPSA Acquires Steel Challenge," December 14, 2007 [Press release].)

Steel Challenge Shooting Association (SCSA) was founded in 1981. At the inaugural event, seventy shooters competed across four stages in an event called the World Speed Shooting Championship. John Shaw won the competition and was the first to be given the title of "World's Fastest Shooter." It was a big moment in the history of shooting sports, as it expanded shooting sports to a broader audience.

Founders Mike Dalton and Mike Fichman set out to create an event that was spectator- and media-friendly, so they came up with an idea to have a large, commercially sponsored steel match. Sometimes referred to as, "drag racing with guns," a speed steel match focuses on speed and precision across multiple steel targets. Dalton and Fichman wanted a simple game that would be exciting to watch and challenging to compete in.

The stage designs are simple, easy-to-follow courses of fire with five steel plates, with one always designated as the "stop plate." At the start signal, competitors use their firearm to engage the five targets, always shooting the stop plate last. The score is determined by the time it takes to hit all five plates, and the lowest time wins.

In 2007, the United States Practical Shooting Association (USPSA) purchased the SCSA Steel Challenge to expand the sport. Today, Steel Challenge has grown into an excellent showcase for the sport and allows all skill levels and ages to compete for precision and speed.

As Mike Dalton said, "We have watched this match grow far beyond what we could have ever imagined 26 years ago. However, we realized that our once small match is now at a point that requires greater resources to move to the next level, and USPSA has the expertise and organizational structure to do just that." (USPSA "USPSA Acquires Steel Challenge," December 14, 2007 [Press release].)

GAME OVERVIEW

Steel Challenge Shooting Association (SCSA) is often just referred to as Steel Challenge. It is a speed shooting competition that is easy to understand and easy to get started. It has a simple set of rules, range commands, and objectives that first-time shooters will comprehend quickly.

When you come to a Steel Challenge match, you will see people of all ages and capabilities enjoying their time with others as they compete. It has something for everyone. It doesn't require a high-speed race gun; you can start with a .22 rifle or .22-caliber pistol. Participants are segmented into similar equipment divisions and age categories to balance the playing field.

There are eight-stage designs that are set up the same way to ensure consistency across multiple competitions. You can review the eight-stage examples here:

https://pistolshootingsports.com/book-bonus

The farthest target is thirty-five yards, and most targets are seventeen to twenty yards out, making it suitable for beginners and experts alike. Steel Challenge competition is a great way to learn and practice your draw, grip, stance, trigger control, transitions, and seeing your sights at speed.

Competitors are scored on how fast they can complete a stage. The winner will have the lowest total time across all stages in a competition. For each run on the stage, only one hit per target is needed using an unlimited number of rounds (called primary targets). The last plate is called the stop plate, and your stage time and score are recorded when you hit this plate.

Stage planning is simple because there are only five targets per stage, and they are all directly in front of you. Targets consist of circles and large rectangular plates, all set at varying distances.

You engage the targets from designated shooting boxes. Only one stage requires you to move horizontally—about six feet, on the clock, to a secondary shooting position to complete the stage.

Steel Challenge is a game of consistency at speed, so whoever has the best skills and makes the fewest number of mistakes wins!

CHAPTER 35
DIVISIONS AND CATEGORIES

SCSA has the most inclusive set of rules when it comes to equipment divisions of firearms and gear. There are thirteen divisions, including variations of pistols, rifles, calibers, optics, and iron sights. Steel Challenge does not use power-factor calculations for scoring like USPSA; therefore, this opens up the competition to more equipment platforms, including rimfire pistols and rifles.

There are differences in start positions for equipment divisions. For instance, centerfire pistols like 9mm, .40 S&W, and .45 ACP start in a holster. Rimfire pistols and rifles using .22LR cartridges start pointing at a "low ready marker" and are transported between stages unloaded, inside a bag, case, or holster.

There are some distinctions in the type of holsters allowed for centerfire pistol competitors (see detail below). Some divisions are permitted to use a race-style holster, and others use a pouch type. Drawing from concealment is not allowed in SCSA competition.

With so many choices, there is a division for everyone. No matter what division you compete in, the uniform stage designs simplify the movement and skills needed for new competitors getting started.

All competitors must declare and comply with the rules for a given division before engaging in a competition. The overviews that follow should help you quickly understand at a high level what each SCSA division is about, but please note that this is not a substitution for a competitor's understanding of the official rules. It is your responsibility to check the official rules and understand them before you compete or make any modifications to your pistol. The official SCSA division rules can be found at https://scsa.org.

CENTERFIRE PISTOL DIVISIONS

Production (PROD) - Production pistols are stock iron or fiber-sighted pistols that use a double-action or safe-action pistol on the USPSA Production list (https://uspsa.org/productionlist).

The idea of Production is to keep the equipment division aligned with the original manufacturer (using no optics, enhanced magazine wells, ports, or muzzle brakes). The Production division is governed by the same rules used in this division under USPSA. The pistol must start in a practical-style, pouch-type holster.

Example - Production (PROD)

Carry Optics (CO) - Carry Optics starts with a Production division platform but requires optical sights mounted on the slide of the pistol. Competitors must not add enhanced magazine wells, barrel ports, or muzzle brakes. Like the Production division above, the Carry Optics division is governed by the same rules used in USPSA (https://uspsa.org/rules), and the pistol must start in a practical-style, pouch-type holster.

Example - Carry Optics (CO)

Iron Sight Revolver (ISR) - Any revolver with iron or fiber-optic sights may be used in this division. There are no restrictions on barrel length or the number of rounds in the cylinder, but it must start in a holster.

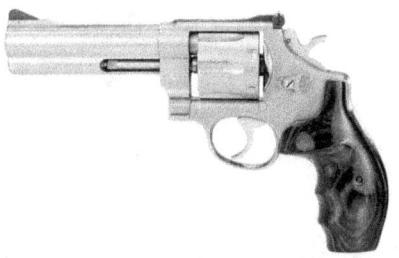

Example - Iron Sight Revolver (ISR)

Optic Sight Revolver (OSR) - This division has the same rules as iron sight revolver but adds an optical or electronic sighting system rather than the standard iron sights.

Example - Optic Sight Revolver (OSR)

Limited (LTD) - The Limited division includes guns that use iron or fiber sights, without optics (electronic sighting systems), ports, or compensators, but may be equipped with other custom features, like upgraded magazine wells, triggers, and internal components. They must start in a race- or practical-style holster.

Example - Limited (LTD)

Open (OPN) - Open guns are considered to be the "racing division" category across all shooting sports, as they can be customized, highly tuned, and expensive when compared to other divisions. Pistols may be equipped with optics mounted to the frame, compensators, barrel ports, brakes, enhanced magazine wells, and internal parts. These guns must also start in a race- or practical-type holster per division rules.

Example - Open (OPN)

Single Stack (SS) - This division covers Single Stack 1911-style pistols with metal frames. This division is governed by the same rules used in the USPSA Single Stack 1911 division (https://uspsa.org/rules). All Single Stack division handguns must start in a practical-style, pouch-type holster.

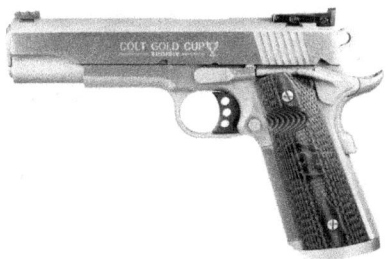

Example - Single Stack (SS)

RIMFIRE PISTOL DIVISIONS

Rimfire Pistol Iron (RFPI) - This division applies to pistols with iron or fiber-optic sights using .22LR ammunition with no compensators or barrel ports. Rimfire pistols are a great way to get started with something low cost that has a very low recoil.

This division does not require the use of a holster, so the starting position is pointing at a low ready marker.

Example - Rimfire Pistol Iron (RFPI)

Rimfire Pistol Open (RFPO) - This division is a race-style division for .22LR pistols. Competitors may use electronic dot optics, compensators, and ported barrels. This division does not require the use of a holster, so the starting position is pointing at a low ready marker.

Example - Rimfire Pistol Open (RFPO)

RIMFIRE RIFLES

Rimfire Rifle Iron (RFRI) - This division applies to all rimfire rifles chambered in .22LR using iron/fiber sights, without barrel ports or compensators. Start position is pointed at a low ready marker.

Example - Rimfire Rifle Iron (RFRI)

Rimfire Rifle Open (RFRO) - This division includes all rimfire rifles chambered in .22LR using electronic optics or red dot sights. Barrel ports and compensators are also permitted. Starting position is pointing at a low ready marker.

Example - Rimfire Rifle Open (RFRO)

PISTOL CALIBER CARBINE DIVISIONS

Pistol Caliber Carbine Irons (PCCI) - This division refers to rifles chambered in centerfire pistol cartridges. Examples include 9mm, .38 Special, .40 S&W/10mm, 357 Sig, or .45 ACP with a maximum velocity of 1,600 FPS. Only fiber-optic or iron sights are allowed, and the starting position is pointing at a low ready marker.

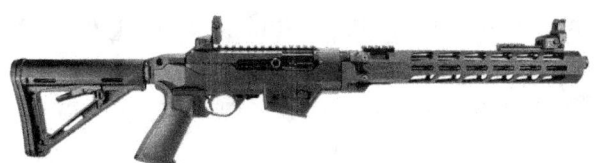

Example - Pistol Caliber Carbine Irons (PCCI)

Pistol Caliber Carbine Open (PCCO) - This division refers to rifles that use a centerfire pistol cartridge chambered in 9mm, .38 Special, .40 S&W/10mm, 357 Sig, or .45 ACP with a maximum bullet velocity of 1,600 FPS. These competitors use red dot and electronic optics, and the starting position is pointing at a low ready marker.

Example - Pistol Caliber Carbine Open (PCCO)

CATEGORIES

Categories are individual segments that create a subset of specific competitors within a match. Categories work great for larger competitions where you have more than one or two people in a given segment.

Categories approved for individual recognition include:

- **Lady** - Female gender as listed on a government-issued ID.
- **Junior** - Competitors under the age of eighteen on the first day of the match.
- **Pre-Teen** - Competitors under thirteen years of age on the first day of the match.
- **Senior** - Competitors must be over the age of fifty-five on the first day of the match.
- **Super Senior** - Competitors must be over the age of sixty-five on the first day of the match.

- **Military** - Competitors must be military personnel on current active-duty orders.
- **Law Enforcement** - Competitors must be full-time law enforcement officers with arrest powers.

Note: All competitors under the age of eighteen must be accompanied by a parent or guardian for the duration of the competition. The parent or guardian must complete a liability waiver for the accompanied minor. When a parent or guardian is competing with a minor, they must be "squaded" (grouped) together. Competitors under the age of eighteen must be able to demonstrate the safe operation and handling of a loaded firearm. See the SCSA site for detailed information on all rules: https://scsa.org.

CHAPTER 36
TARGETS AND STAGES

TARGETS

In Steel Challenge, all plates are the same color and usually painted white. The stop plate is designated by painting the two-by-four post with a color (usually red, orange, or black). The post color makes the stop plate quickly stand out from the rest of the four targets.

There are only three types of plates used in a Steel Challenge competition.

- 18-by-24-inch rectangle plate
- 10-inch round plate
- 12-inch round plate

Target heights are consistent for each stage except for two targets on the pendulum stage. The pendulum stage has two round, twelve-inch targets that are six feet from the top of the target to the ground. Rectangle targets are five feet, six inches from the top of the plate to the ground, and round targets are set five feet high from the top of the target to the ground.

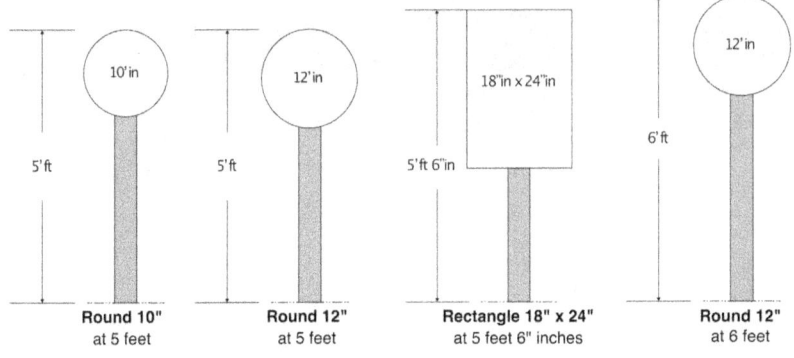

Steel Challenge - Match targets and dimensions

STAGES

When you attend a Steel Challenge match, you will see that there are only eight official stages. Each stage has five plates at distances of seven to thirty-five yards. You always shoot the same eight stages so you can easily practice outside of match competition.

Each run or string gets timed, and your cumulative times become your score. The competitor with the lowest overall cumulative score wins. A minimum of four scored stages per division are required to receive a classification.

Steel Challenge competitions are very much a mental game of consistency and performance. It helps to have a plan when shooting any stage. Review the stage diagrams so you understand where you will shoot first and where you will finish on the stop plate.

The table below is an example of an eight-stage competition where you shoot multiple strings per stage.

Stage Identifier	Stage Name	Strings	Max Distance	Notes
SC-101	Five to Go	4 of 5	18 yds	1 shooting box
SC-102	Showdown	4 of 5	25 yds	2 shooting boxes 3 strings from 1 box and 2 strings from the other
SC-103	Smoke & Hope	4 or 5	14 yds	1 shooting box Fastest Stage Times
SC-104	Outer Limits	3 of 4	35 yds	The only stage with 3 shooting boxes and movement under time
SC-105	Accelerator	4 of 5	20 yds	1 shooting box
SC-106	The Pendulum	4 of 5	18 yds	1 shooting box
SC-107	Speed Option	4 of 5	35 yds	1 shooting box
SC-108	Roundabout	4 of 5	17 yds	1 shooting box

Because rimfire pistols and rifles can be used and don't require holsters, it is a great way to get new people started in the sport. Shooting steel targets is a fun way to learn about competitions because each hit on steel gives you instant feedback.

For additional book bonus material on Steel Challenge, see the companion website at:

https://pistolshootingsports.com/book-bonus.

CHAPTER 37
SC-101 FIVE TO GO

Five to Go is four 10-inch round steel plate targets set at 5 feet high and each plate is progressively farther than the previous. The stop plate is a quick transition to the right on a 12-inch plate set at 7 yards. Engage (T1-T4) Finish on Stop Plate (SP) - Competitors shoot all five strings from the center shooting box. Best four of five runs count for score.

Targets and Shooting Boxes:

- One 3-by-3 shooting box at the centerline
- Four 10-inch plates at 5 feet high
- One 12-inch stop plate (SP) at 5 feet high

Target Distances

- 18 yards deep (firing line to farthest target)
- 27 feet, 4 inches wide (left to right from target centers)
- Average target distance = 12.4 yards

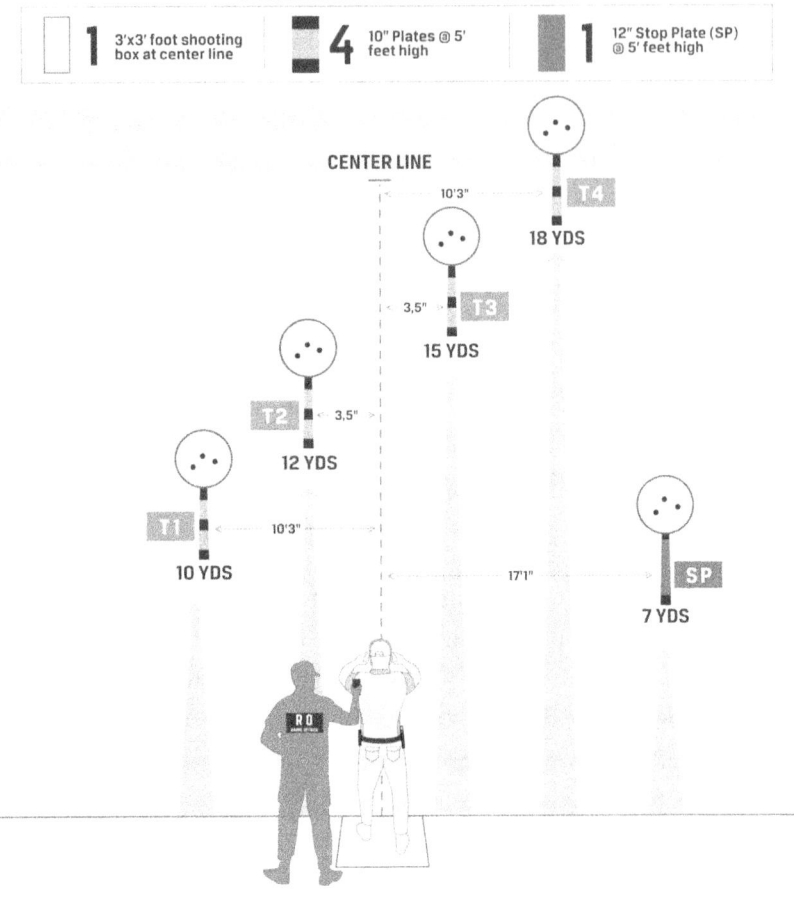

CHAPTER 38
SC-102 SHOWDOWN

Showdown is a five string stage with two shooting locations. The two shooting locations create a different challenge across the same targets. Engage (T1-T4) Finish on Stop Plate (SP) - Competitors shoot three strings from one shooting box and two strings from the other with no more than three strings from any one box. There is no movement between boxes during a string.

Targets and Shooting Boxes:

- Two 3-by-3 shooting boxes 6 feet apart
- Two 10-inch plates at 5 feet high
- Two 18-by-24-inch rectangles at 5 feet, 6 inches high
- One 12-inch stop plate (SP) at 5 feet high

Max Target Distances:

- 25 yards deep (firing line to farthest target)
- 18 feet wide (left to right from target centers)
- Average target distance = 16.4 yards

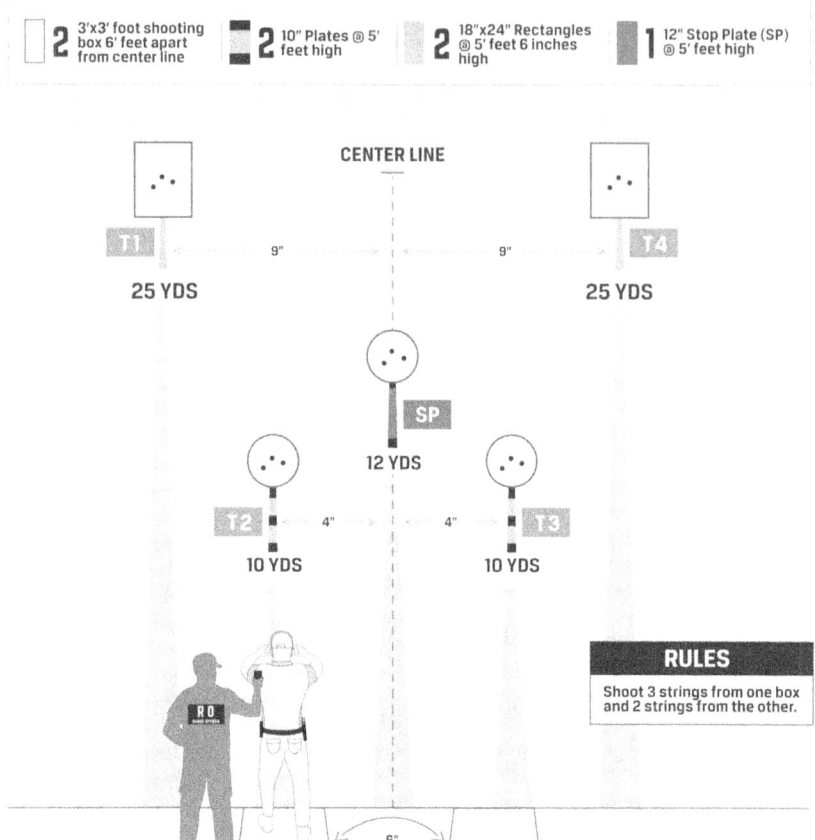

CHAPTER 39
SC-103 SMOKE & HOPE

Smoke & Hope is close distance fast shooting with fast transitions on large targets. Engage (T1-T4) Finish on Stop Plate (SP) - Competitors shoot five strings from one shooting box. Best four out of five runs count for score.

Targets and Shooting Boxes:

- One 3-by-3 shooting box at the centerline
- Four 18-by-24-inch rectangles at 5 feet, 6 inches high
- One 12-inch stop plate (SP) at 5 feet high

Max Target Distances:

- 14 yards deep (firing line to farthest target)
- 28 feet wide (left to right from target centers)
- Average target distance = 9.2 yards

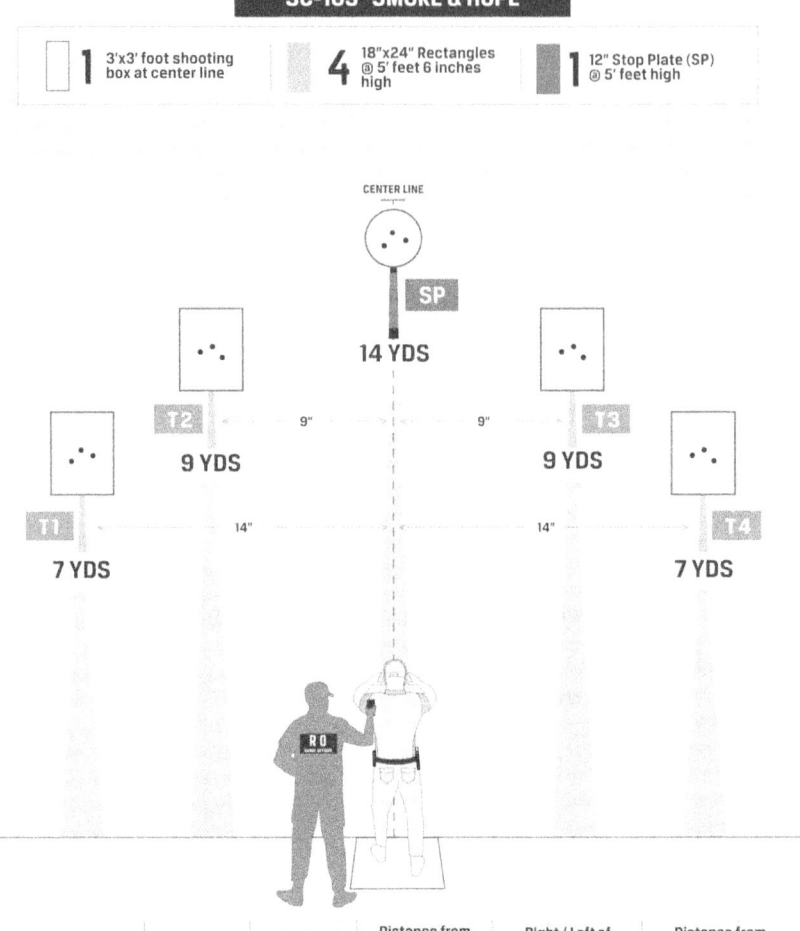

CHAPTER 40
SC-104 OUTER LIMITS

Outer Limits is the only stage in Steel Challenge where movement is part of your timed performance. Remember to keep your firearm pointed down range and your finger out of the trigger guard as you move to the second position.

Engage (T1-T4) Finish on Stop Plate (SP) - Competitors shoot four strings, starting from their respective weak-side shooting box. Right-handed shooters will begin from the left, and left-handed shooters will start from the right. Competitors start by engaging the two targets on their starting side of the centerline, then move to the center shooting box, under time, to complete the remaining three targets. Note that any single competitor will use only two of the three boxes. The best three out of four runs count for the overall score.

Targets and Shooting Boxes:

- Three 4-by-4 shooting boxes 6 feet apart
- Two 12-inch plates at 5 feet high
- Two 18-by-24-inch rectangles at 5 feet, 6 inches high
- One 12-inch stop plate (SP) at 5 feet high

Max Target Distances:

- 35 yards deep (firing line to farthest target)
- 24 feet wide (left to right from target centers)
- Average target distance = 25.6 yards

SC-104 OUTER LIMITS

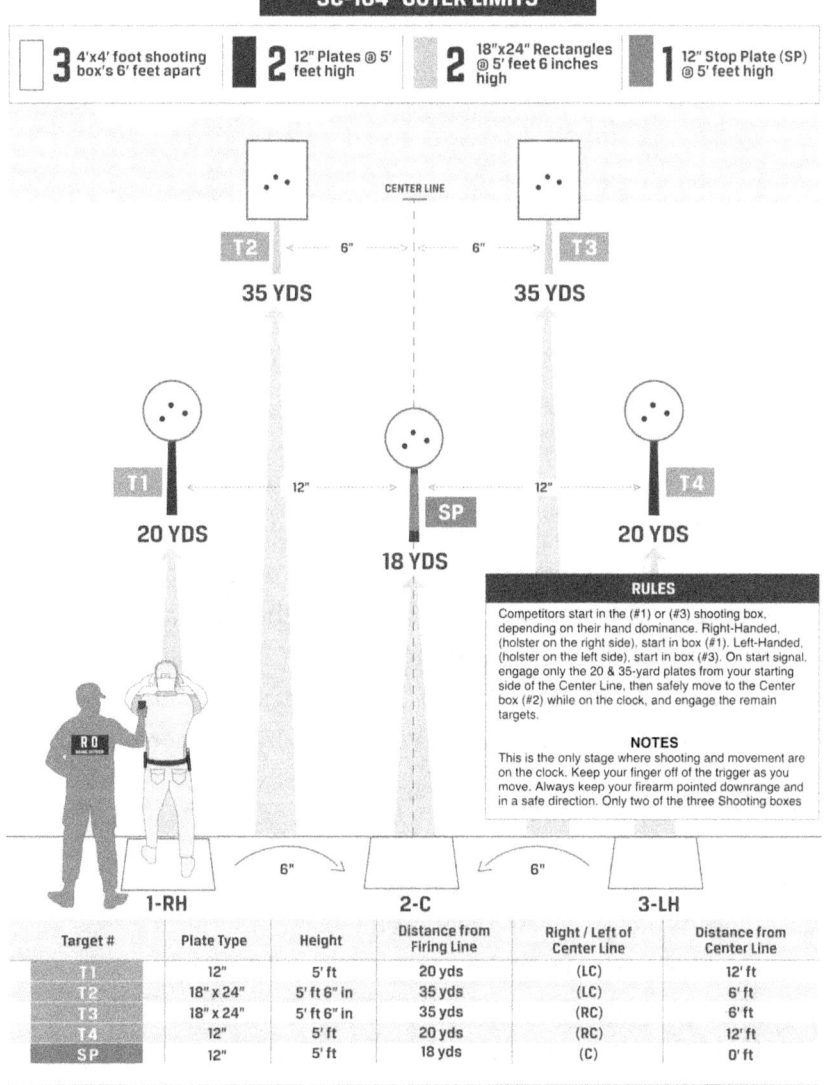

3 4'x4' foot shooting box's 6' feet apart
2 12" Plates @ 5' feet high
2 18"x24" Rectangles @ 5' feet 6 inches high
1 12" Stop Plate (SP) @ 5' feet high

RULES

Competitors start in the (#1) or (#3) shooting box, depending on their hand dominance. Right-Handed, (holster on the right side), start in box (#1). Left-Handed, (holster on the left side), start in box (#3). On start signal, engage only the 20 & 35-yard plates from your starting side of the Center Line, then safely move to the Center box (#2) while on the clock, and engage the remain targets.

NOTES

This is the only stage where shooting and movement are on the clock. Keep your finger off of the trigger as you move. Always keep your firearm pointed downrange and in a safe direction. Only two of the three Shooting boxes

Target #	Plate Type	Height	Distance from Firing Line	Right / Left of Center Line	Distance from Center Line
T1	12"	5' ft	20 yds	(LC)	12' ft
T2	18" x 24"	5' ft 6" in	35 yds	(LC)	6' ft
T3	18" x 24"	5' ft 6" in	35 yds	(RC)	6' ft
T4	12"	5' ft	20 yds	(RC)	12' ft
SP	12"	5' ft	18 yds	(C)	0' ft

Max Target Distances: 35 yards deep - (Firing line to farthest target) 24 feet wide - (farthest distance left to right from target centers)

Stage Scoring: Best 3 of 5 runs

CHAPTER 41
SC-105 ACCELERATOR

Accelerator is a good mix of shooting near and far as you transition from the two closest targets to the two farthest before finishing on the center stop plate. Engage (T1-T4) Finish on Stop Plate (SP) - Competitors shoot all five strings from the center shooting box. Best four out of five runs count for score.

Targets and Shooting Boxes:

- One 3-by-3 shooting box at the centerline
- One 10-inch plate at 5 feet high
- One 12-inch plate at 5 feet high
- Two 18-by-24-inch rectangles at 5 feet, 6 inches high
- One 12-inch stop plate (SP) at 5 feet high

Max Target Distances:

- 20 yards deep (firing line to farthest target)
- 32 feet wide (left to right from target centers)
- Average target distance = 15 yards

SC-105 ACCELERATOR

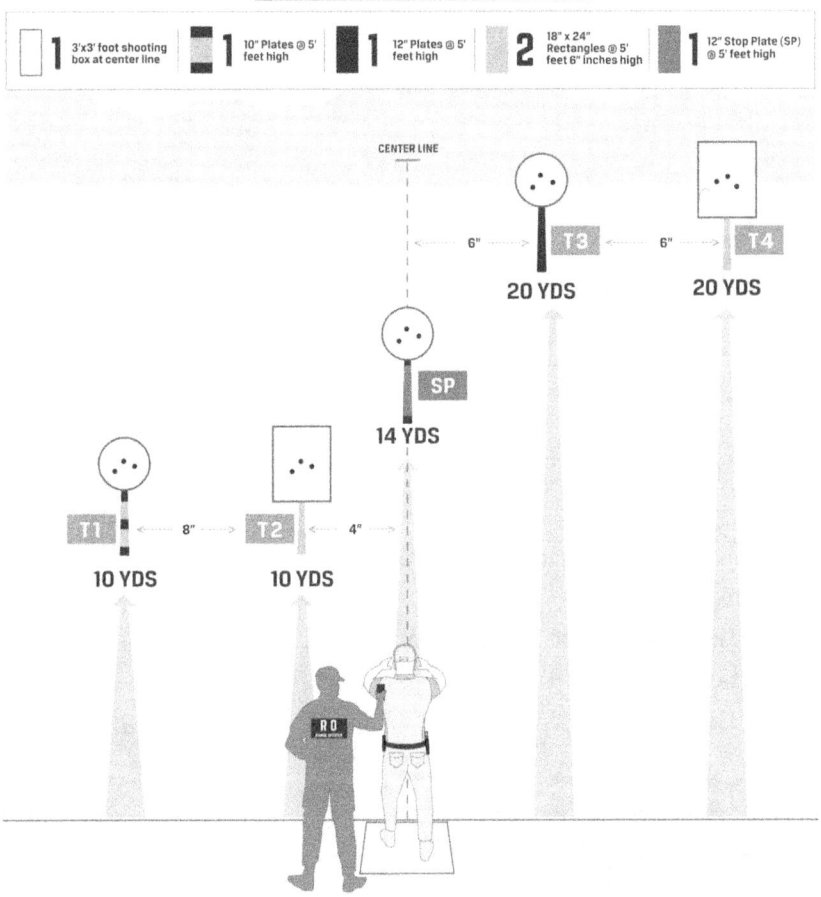

Target #	Plate Type	Height	Distance from Firing Line	Right / Left of Center Line	Distance from Center Line
T1	10"	5' ft	10 yds	(LC)	12' ft
T2	18" x 24"	5' ft 6" in	10 yds	(LC)	4' ft
T3	12"	5' ft	20 yds	(RC)	6' ft
T4	18" x 24"	5' ft 6" in	20 yds	(RC)	20' ft
SP	12"	5' ft	15 yds	C	0' ft

Max Target Distances: 20 yards deep - (Firing line to farthest target) 32 feet wide - (farthest distance left to right from target centers)

Stage Scoring: Best 4 of 5 runs

CHAPTER 42
SC-106 PENDULUM

Pendulum is distance shooting across four plates at 18 yards. It requires good sight pictures and transitions. Engage (T1-T4) Finish on Stop Plate (SP) - Competitors shoot all five strings from the center shooting box. Best four out of five runs count for score.

Targets and Shooting Boxes:

- One 3-by-3 shooting box at centerline
- Two 10-inch plates at 5 feet high
- Two 12-inch plates at 6 feet high
- One 12-inch stop plate (SP) at 5 feet high

Max Target Distances:

- 18 yards deep (firing line to farthest target)
- 24 feet wide (farthest distance, left to right, from target centers)
- Average target distance = 16.4 yards

SC-106 PENDULUM

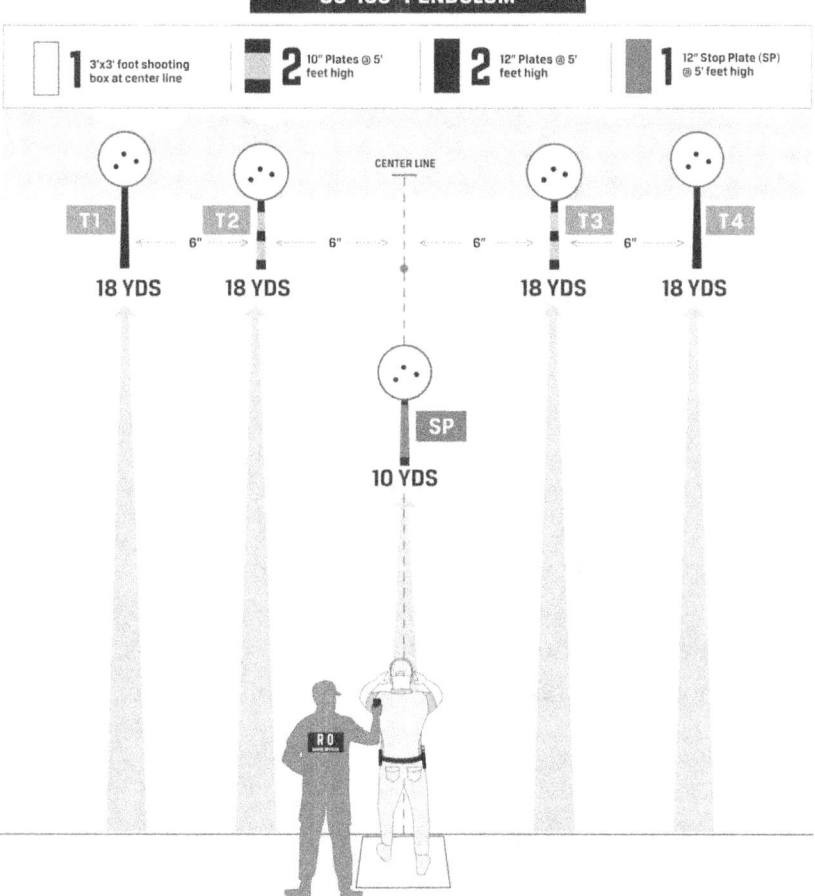

- **1** 3'x3' foot shooting box at center line
- **2** 10" Plates @ 5' feet high
- **2** 12" Plates @ 5' feet high
- **1** 12" Stop Plate (SP) @ 5' feet high

Target #	Plate Type	Height	Distance from Firing Line	Right / Left of Center Line	Distance from Center Line
T1	12"	6' ft	18 yds	(LC)	12' ft / 0" in
T2	10"	5' ft	18 yds	(LC)	6' ft / 0" in
T3	10"	5' ft	18 yds	(RC)	6' ft / 0" in
T4	12"	6' ft	18 yds	(RC)	12' ft / 0" in
SP	12"	5' ft	10 yds	C	0' ft / 0" in

Max Target Distances: 18 yards deep - (Firing line to farthest target)   24 feet wide - (farthest distance left to right from target centers)

Stage Scoring: Best 4 of 5 runs

CHAPTER 43
SC-107 SPEED OPTION

Speed Option tests shooting at multiple distances and has the farthest stop plate of all the stages. Engage (T1-T4) Finish on Stop Plate (SP) - Competitors shoot all five strings from the center shooting box. Best four out of five runs count for score.

Targets and Shooting Boxes:

- One 3-by-3 shooting box at the centerline
- Four 12-inch plates at 5 feet high
- One 18-by-24-inch rectangle (SP) at 5 feet, 6 inches high

Max Target Distances:

- 35 yards deep (firing line to farthest target)
- 42 feet, 5 inches wide (farthest distance, left to right, from target centers)
- Average target distance = 17.6 yards

SC-107 SPEED OPTION

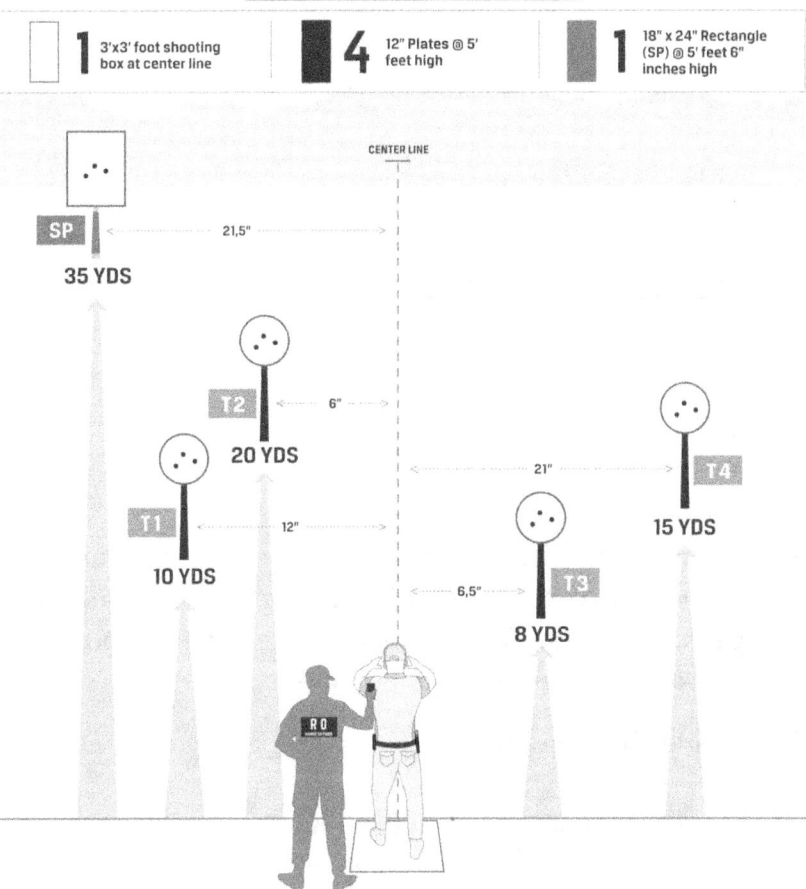

Target #	Plate Type	Height	Distance from Firing Line	Right / Left of Center Line	Distance from Center Line
T1	12"	5' ft	10 yds	(LC)	12' ft
T2	12"	5' ft	20 yds	(LC)	6' ft
T3	12"	5' ft	8 yds	(RC)	6' ft / 5" in
T4	12"	5' ft	15 yds	(RC)	21' ft
SP	18" x 24"	5' ft 6" in	35 yds	(LC)	21' ft / 5" in

Max Target Distances: 35 yards deep - (Firing line to farthest target) 42 feet wide - (farthest distance left to right from target centers)

Stage Scoring: Best 4 of 5 runs

CHAPTER 44
SC-108 ROUNDABOUT

Roundabout is four 12-inch near and far targets surrounding a 12-inch stop plate. Engage (T1-T4) Finish on Stop Plate (SP) - Competitors shoot all five strings from the center shooting box. Best four out of five runs count for score.

Targets and Shooting Boxes:

- One 3-by-3 shooting box at the centerline
- Four 12-inch plates at 5 feet high
- One 12-inch stop plate (SP) at 5 feet high

Max Target Distances:

- 15 yards deep (firing line to farthest target)
- 17 feet wide (farthest distance, left to right, from target centers)
- Average target distance = 10.8 yards

SC-108 ROUNDABOUT

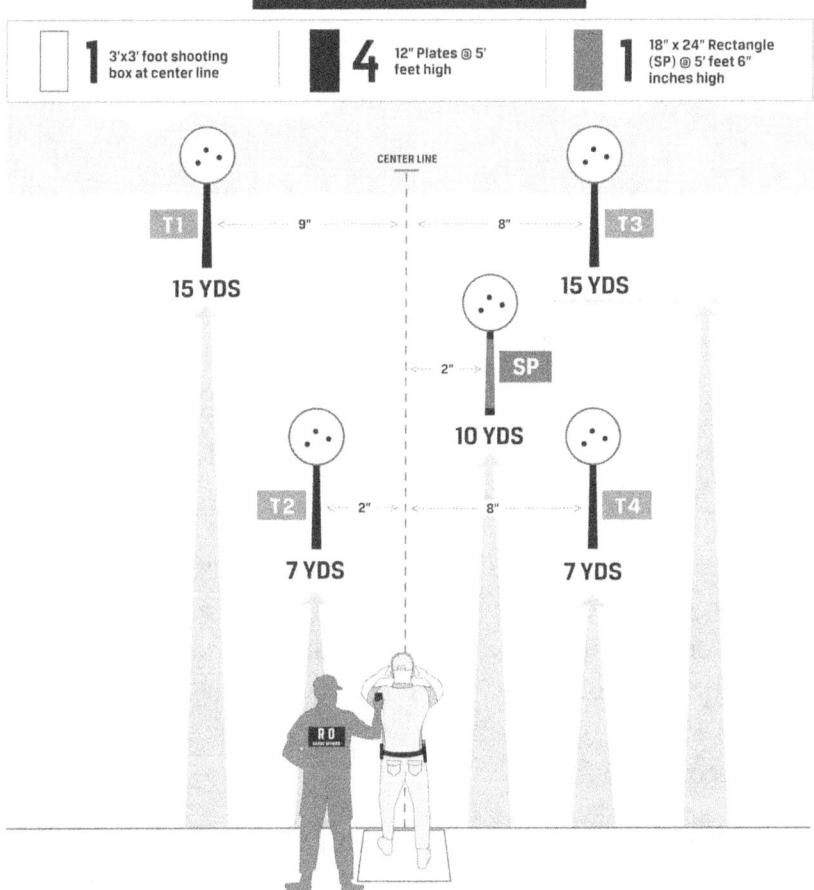

1 3'x3' foot shooting box at center line

4 12" Plates @ 5' feet high

1 18" x 24" Rectangle (SP) @ 5' feet 6" inches high

Target #	Plate Type	Height	Distance from Firing Line	Right / Left of Center Line	Distance from Center Line
T1	12"	5' ft	15 yds	(LC)	9' ft
T2	12"	5' ft	7 yds	(LC)	2' ft
T3	12"	5' ft	15 yds	(RC)	8' ft
T4	12"	5' ft	7 yds	(RC)	8' ft
SP	12"	5' ft	10 yds	(RC)	2' ft

Max Target Distances: 15 yards deep - (Firing line to farthest target) 17 feet wide - (farthest distance left to right from target centers)

Stage Scoring: Best 4 of 5 runs

CHAPTER 45
SCORING AND CLASSIFICATION

Scoring a Steel Challenge match is straightforward. You shoot each stage for the fastest times. Your worst string time will be thrown out on each stage, and the total remaining string times, subtracting any penalties, will be your score for that stage. The total of all your stage scores is your match score. The lowest match score wins.

Competitors may use as many rounds as needed to hit all five plates, as long as it's within thirty seconds. The maximum time on any stage is thirty seconds. This limit helps keep things moving in case of equipment issues. Scoring timers signal the start of your run with an audible beep, then use the sound of each shot to record elapsed time. Your final shot marks your overall stage time.

Penalties: It is important to hit every plate, and makeup shots are highly encouraged. If you shoot the stop plate before you hit all the other plates, each missed plate will add a three-second penalty to your overall time on that string. Keep both feet inside the designated shooting box whenever you are engaging targets because any shot fired with one or both feet outside of the shooting box results in a three-second penalty per shot.

Reliability and Speed

Use rounds that correctly and consistently cycle your firearm, as this will help you lay down your fastest times. Many of the best competitors practice with the same ammunition in order to achieve a consistent feel with the cycling and timing of their firearm.

Classification

Classification is a great way to track your overall performance, measure improvements, and compare your performance against other competitors. The SCSA (Steel Challenge) classification system is different from the USPSA classification system, as only official SCSA stage classifiers are used for SCSA classification.

Sanctioned Competition

In sanctioned competitions, there will be at least four official stages in order for an official score to be submitted for a division classification. If you would like to participate in the classification system, you will need to become a member of USPSA/SCSA. Your membership number enables your match performance scores to be tracked through the system.

When you compete in sanctioned matches, your scores will be uploaded and linked to your membership number. After shooting several matches in a particular division, the tracking system will begin to rank competitors by their lowest (fastest) time on each stage using the classification calculation (see below).

Division Baselines

Every SCSA division has a set of eight peak stage times (PSTs) that represent baseline performances for each stage. These peak stage times represent the best scores recorded, reviewed, and published for an evaluation period. PSTs are reviewed yearly and updated as needed.

You can look at stage PSTs to see how your performance compares to the best scores in that division. Reviewing PSTs will help you understand which stages you can practice more to increase your overall classification. Your classification is calculated by looking at your classifier stage times and the PSTs on each classifier for your division.

Scoring Example: If you are shooting in the Limited division, and you score 105 in a match of all eight stages, you would take the current eight published PSTs for each stage in the Limited division and add them up.

Let's say the current PSTs total is 90. Your classification for that match would be: PST / Your Score = Your Match Performance Classification or 90 / 105 = 85.71%. This would place you in the Master (M) classification for that match.

The classification system will use your best classifier stage scores across several matches. The more competitions you enter, the more likely your classification will improve.

The most current peak stage times (PSTs) for each division and classifier stage are found here: https://scsa.org.

Steel Challenge Shooting Association (SCSA) Classification Scale

- Grand Master >=95%
- Master >=85%
- A Class >=75%
- B Class >=60%
- C Class >=40%
- D Class <=39%

· · ·

Evaluating performance

There are a couple ways to assess your performance. One is to record your best times in a journal so you can review and take notes on your individual stage runs and classifier scores. This will help you understand what classifiers you excel at and which ones need more practice. As you keep a journal, you get to see all your incremental performance improvements over time. The other way to look at your performance is at a division level. You can compare your individual stage classifier scores to other competitors shooting in the same division.

Note: Unlike USPSA competitions, power factor and hit factor calculations are not used in Steel Challenge. See the power factor and hit factor sections in the USPSA chapter.

CHAPTER 46
STARTING POSITIONS AND STRATEGY

STARTING POSITIONS

Whenever a competitor is in the shooting box and the range officer has given the command to "make ready," you must always keep the muzzle of the firearm pointed downrange. The following provides more details on starting positions depending on the type of firearm used.

Centerfire Pistols - Wrists Above Shoulders

Centerfire pistols use a holster, and the starting position is "wrists above shoulders." This position is also called a "surrender start." Your wrists must be visible to everyone behind you. It helps to create a consistent index for these kinds of starts, like touching your hearing protection or the rim of your hat. Using the same hand positions at the beginning will help develop consistency as you move from the starting position to your pistol grip.

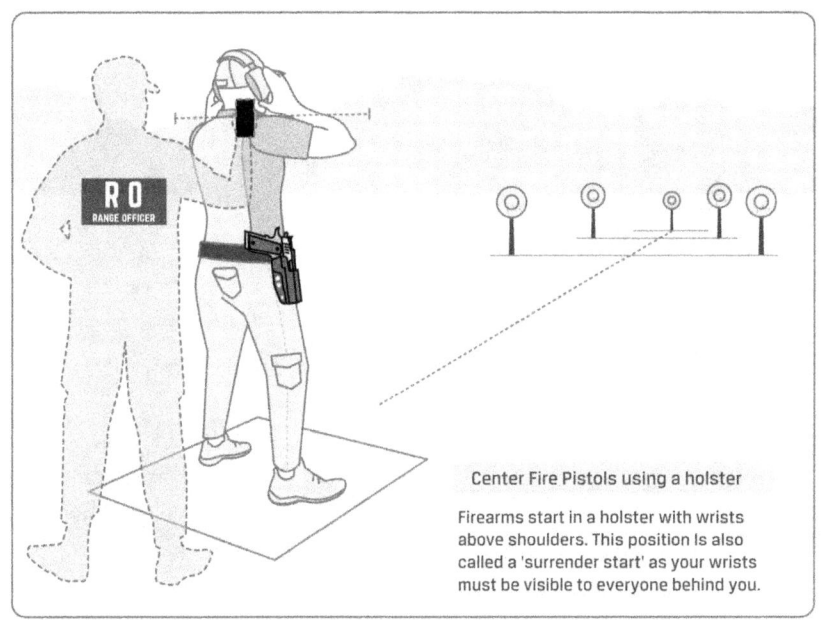

Wrists Above Shoulders

Rimfire Pistols and all Rifles - Low Ready

For rimfire pistols and rifles, you will make ready and point your firearm at the designated aiming point. This point is usually a safety cone, flag, or sign that is centered downrange ten feet from the shooting-box start position. Always keep the firearm pointed downrange and your finger off the trigger until you are ready to fire.

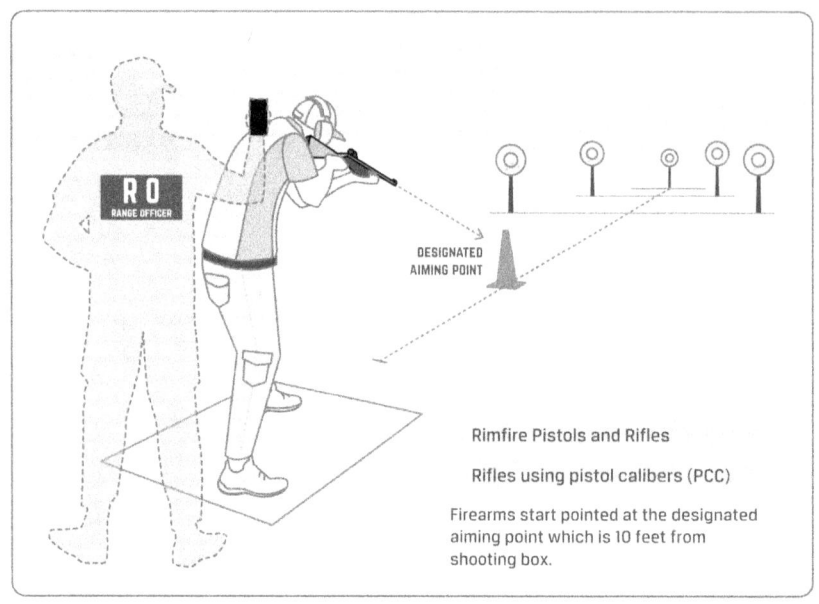

Low Ready Position

Remember, when you have settled in and stopped moving, this is the signal to the range officer (RO) that you are ready to start your run.

STRATEGY

The SCSA game is high speed, yet simple. Mental consistency is essential to performance runs at the highest level. Be conscious of what you are thinking about before you start each stage and string. Stay focused in order to do your best. You will only get faster and more proficient the more stages you shoot. When you start competing in larger matches, it quickly comes down to the least number of mistakes and greatest efficiencies that win the game.

• • •

Fundamentals

Ensure you have a good grip for the first shot because everything moves very quickly from there. Prepare the trigger on the transition to your next target and know how your sight picture should look and what you need to see on near and far targets to hit them. Longer shots will always require the best technique, grip, trigger preparation, and sight pictures. It is also imperative to keep the gun up after you draw, during transitions, and when you move to a second shooting position on the "Outer Limits" stage.

Efficiency

Look for and practice ways to accomplish efficiency gains. One of the best ways to be more efficient is to focus on your transition times. If you were to focus on transitions and improve your individual runs by 0.25 seconds, you will have improved your stage score by 1.0 second for a four-string stage. Seconds saved on each stage add up across a multistage match and matter even more as you look at overall scores. Look for all the different ways you can be more efficient and lower your stage times.

Consistency

A consistent draw is essential, as it is the sequence where you establish your grip and initial sight picture on a target. When you get your grip and first shot right, it helps create momentum for the rest of your stage run.

Centerfire pistol competitors should train consistently to smoothly execute that first shot on target from a surrender draw position. As you practice the surrender draw, place your wrists above each respective shoulder and touch your hat or ear protection to establish a consistent starting position.

You want to minimize excessive movement where you can. Some competitors find it's easier to work backward from the gun on target to the surrender position so they can review each step. This helps to confirm the motions in both directions. You can practice this several times, paying attention to the movement that works best and enables you to execute the draw consistently.

Reaction Time

When you get consistent with drawing and shooting fundamentals, start reviewing your reaction times from the start signal. Practice your reaction time and draw to first shot in dry-fire using a par timer. Your reaction time plus draw time can contribute a significant portion to your overall stage times. Focus on a crisp, clean, smooth draw stroke. In the course of an eight-stage match, you will perform thirty-nine draws. The draw is a large part of your score, so practice it.

Take deep breaths before you begin. Don't rush things in practice. Look for ways to be consistent that will help your performance. The shortest distance to something is usually the most direct, so look for any places where you can reduce or eliminate excessive movements.

Routine

Develop a pre-engagement and make-ready routine that you can follow every time. Your pre-engagement routine should start when you are the next person up to compete. Clear your head and think about what you are going to do. It helps to visualize as much as you can. See the targets in the order you will engage them from the shooting box. Visualize as much detail as you can about your sight pictures, target order, and making that perfect run. Listen to the RO's commands before it's your turn on the stage. Some people do this with eyes closed, as it helps them visualize better.

Check your grip and dry your palms if needed. If you have sweaty hands, use a grip aid like Pro Grip, chalk, or dirt to keep them dry and ensure a good grip.

Know where you are going to stand in the box before you get there. If you need to move on a stage, get close to the side where you will be moving from and count the number of steps required to get inside the second shooting box. After the RO gives the "make ready" command, establish a sight picture on each target, load, and move into your start position.

Get your first run in the bag by focusing on hitting all the targets on the first shot with clean transitions. Having a clean first run will help get you focused and the momentum going in the right direction.

After you complete a stage, get in the habit of topping off your magazines so that you are not caught off guard when you are on deck for the next stage. Verifying that you have enough working magazines before each stage helps you to focus on the other things that will give you a better score. It always helps to have five magazines so you can get a fresh one for each string as needed. You don't want to put yourself in a position where you need to perform a reload during your stage run in order to complete it.

Saving Time

As you shoot and become classified in a division, you will want to look at ways to improve your classification. Saving a few tenths of a second here and there will go a long way toward improving your overall scores.

Practice drills in dry-fire using a par timer. Use a journal to record your best times on classifiers and any notes you observe. The information you record in a journal will help inform you of the places where you can save time.

Draws and transitions are a great place to look for improvements, as they are the only time you are not firing the gun. Practice drawing and shooting targets at different distances to see what is needed to hit the target in the shortest time. You may discover that to avoid misses on far targets, you need a few more tenths of a second to focus on a good sight picture and prepping the trigger.

It is good to know what your shot-to-shot transition times are for each target on a stage. You can test your transition skills in practice, shooting targets in different orders. You may see that certain right-to-left or left-to-right transitions give you faster times. Tracking your performance will teach you a lot about your shooting.

Pick any stage, keep it simple, and start recording your times and any other observations you have about your practice. In the end, it will be all the little things you improved on that will boost your performance and score.

Makeup Shots

Missing a target and shooting the stop plate gives you a three-second penalty. However, if you can make up the missed plate in less than three seconds, it will improve your score. It is always better to hit the target the first time and take the time needed to see what you need to see in order to make a good shot.

CHAPTER 47
TRAINING AND RESOURCES

When training, it is good to break down each part of your performance, then measure where you are at and where you can improve. Use a shot timer so you can see the places where you spend the most time. If you have adjustable sights, make sure you zero them so you are not trying to figure them out during a training session or competition.

Create a practice schedule that you can stick to for several weeks and follow through with consistently. Use the same equipment (pistol and ammunition) so you do not introduce inconsistencies. Practice with the shot timer to develop better reaction times to the start signal and constantly measure your drill performance.

When you're starting, you don't always need to be the fastest in every drill—rather, it is more desirable to deliver a consistent performance. Going too fast and needing to take makeup shots will cost you extra time. Make sure you see what you need to see with your sights and execute good trigger control as you practice.

It helps to look at a target first and then bring the gun to the point where you are looking.

Draw Speed to the First Target

Your draw is a significant contributor to your overall stage time in Steel Challenge. It will help you to measure how long it takes to draw and get your first shot on target at all seven specific distances. Record your times so you can see where you need to practice. Hitting the target with proper technique rather than being the fastest is the goal for these live-fire drills.

You will need three practice targets (a 10-inch plate, a 12-inch plate, and a 18-by-24-inch rectangle). If you don't have steel plates, use paper targets. Practice drawing and shooting at these targets from the seven distances (listed below), just like you would see them on a stage. You will understand just what kind of sight picture is needed to hit them at each distance. The longer distances and smaller targets will require a better sight picture and your best technique.

Draw to First Target - Accuracy at Speed drills

- 7 yards, 18-by-24-inch rectangle (Smoke & Hope)
- 10 yards, 10-inch plate (Five to Go/Accelerator)
- 15 yards, 12-inch plate (Speed Option/Roundabout)
- 18 yards, 12-inch plate, 6 feet high (Pendulum)
- 20 yards, 12-inch plate (Outer Limits)
- 25 yards, 18-by-24-inch rectangle (Showdown)
- 35 yards, 18-by-24-inch rectangle (Outer Limits)

As you practice, check to see that you are building your grip consistently and observe your natural point of aim, because you want to bring the pistol to the same place each time you draw.

If you need to work more on fundamentals, practice gun manipulations in dry-fire before heading back out to the range. Dry-fire is a great way to work on your grip, draw, presentation, and pistol manipulations. Dry-fire works well when you can follow a routine where you practice for a dedicated period more than once a week. Start with three training sessions of ten minutes and build from there.

Use your shot timer to set par times and measure your reaction to the start timer. Think about starting your draw at the very first sound of the timer and get your dominant hand to make contact before the start signal ends. There are several good books on dry-firing to which you can refer for more information: https://pistolshootingsports.com/book-bonus.

Transitions

As you are only placing one shot on each target, and the time it takes to perform this action is recorded, transitions are a good measure of how long it takes you to:

- Get your eyes on the next target.
- Move the gun into position.
- See a good sight picture.
- Execute proper trigger control.
- Break the shot.

Transition Drills

A great way to isolate work on transitions is to start by setting up three twelve-inch plate targets at the same distance of fifteen yards and five feet apart. Review the split times between each shot. Start by getting a few consistent runs in to get a baseline of your performance, then try to improve your transition times by just getting your eyes on the next target faster.

Increase the distance of the three targets to twenty yards and try the drill again. Record your times and notice what is needed to hit targets at this distance. Increase the distance one last time to twenty-five yards. This distance should take the longest of the three drills and requires better sight pictures and trigger control.

Try "Five to Go" as a practice drill. This stage is one of the best ways to test your transition speed. Each shot gets a little harder as the distance increases, so you will need to ensure better sight pictures, focus, and technique as you shoot through the targets.

It helps to review your performance times after a training session so you can see where you are making progress. Remember, it's always the person with the most consistent performance that excels faster. Train to be consistent.

Book Bonus

For additional book bonus material on Steel Challenge, see the companion website at:

https://pistolshootingsports.com/book-bonus.

PART VII
USPSA COMPETITION
UNITED STATES PRACTICAL SHOOTING ASSOCIATION

CHAPTER 48
HISTORY AND GAME OVERVIEW

HISTORY

Practical shooting sports were established from the need to find better methods and tools on how to effectively use and train with handguns. It also brought people together from different backgrounds in order to share best practices and skills.

Its competitive roots are credited to the competitions that were held in the 1950s in Big Bear, California. These events were known as "leather slap" quick draw events which grew to encompass shooting scenarios and demonstrations of skill that challenged competitors' abilities. People from law enforcement, military, and firearm enthusiasts came together to share, learn, and compete.

As a result of the sport's growth, in 1976, the International Practical Shooting Confederation (IPSC) was formed in Columbia, Missouri. Then in 1984, the United States Practical Shooting Association (USPSA) was created under the IPSC. Today, the USPSA is a thriving organization, where people from all types of backgrounds participate and enjoy shooting sports.

GAME OVERVIEW

The United States Practical Shooting Association (USPSA) is the largest governing organization for practical shooting competitors in the United States. The organization provides the framework for competitions to operate effectively at local, regional, and national levels. The organization manages membership, rules, and governance to conduct effective contests. USPSA hosts yearly national events that bring the best division competitors together in order to compete for the national title.

Practical shooting competitions are organized around several freestyle scenarios (or stages) that contestants solve and score following USPSA rules. The rule format allows stage designers to create challenging stages that test competitors' abilities and ensure safe, fair, and fun competition. Competitions test contestants' abilities to think and resolve the stage challenges quickly.

There are two basic types of stages: match stages and classifier stages. Match stages create unique challenges for competitors to solve. Classifier stages are a consistent test which can be compared at a national level to evaluate performance. Each stage type tests the competitors' skills and expertise in the use of a firearm. USPSA competitors are always trying to improve on their best scores.

Principles

USPSA follows a straightforward set of principles to ensure safety, consistency, and quality of competition. These include the following:

- **Safety** - All matches and courses of fire must be designed with safety in mind.
- **Quality** - Quality is reflected by testing competitors' shooting skills and their physical abilities.

- **Balance** - Speed, power, and accuracy are given equal weighting in course design so competitors may be evaluated equally.
- **Diversity** - Diverse and unique challenges are presented to competitors.
- **Freestyle** - Competitors are allowed to problem-solve on the stage. Standards and classifiers are specific, so competitors' skills can be evaluated across different events.
- **Difficulty** - Each match should present varying levels of difficulty, but must also allow for variance in competitors' physical differences (i.e., their build and height).
- **Challenge** - Competitors are allowed to compete using different firearm systems that are grouped similarly by equipment divisions, calibers, and power factor to ensure consistent competition.
- **Scenarios and Stage Props** - Scenarios and stage props are encouraged to keep the contest exciting without distracting from the challenges or creating unsafe conditions.

The Sport

USPSA is an open sport that encourages responsible and safe firearm handling. The sport creates a competitive environment to equally measure a competitor's ability to master accuracy, power, and speed. The following section is meant to introduce USPSA concepts. Subsequent chapters will use examples to help you understand the details.

String/Stage/Match

- **Strings** are separately timed segments within a stage. Strings might test how well you shoot three targets with your dominant hand for one string, and then test how well you do with your supporting hand for the second string. The two string performances are combined to get an overall stage score.

- **Stages** are scored competitions that present a unique challenge for each competitor to solve. They have specific stage rules for starting position, stage procedures, scoring rules, and placement of targets. Stage designers present different problems through stage design for competitors to solve using their skills and experience.
- **Matches** are multiple stages that make up an event. Depending on the format, match events can be completed in one day or spread out over multiple days. A match score is the sum of a competitor's total stage performances. The best overall score is the match winner.

Scoring

Understanding how scoring works will help inform your ability to plan and shoot an effective strategy. Scoring breaks down into four calculations:

- Power Factor
- Hit Factor
- Stage Points
- Match Points

Power Factor

Power factor measures the power of the bullet load you are shooting from your firearm. There are two classifications: major and minor. Major power loads generate more recoil and are harder to control as you shoot multiple shots in a row. Minor loads generate less recoil and can be softer shooting, so they are easier to get back on target. Power factor is calculated by taking the weight of the bullet, multiplying it by the velocity, then dividing by 1,000. Major power factor starts at 165, and minor starts at 125.

USPSA cardboard targets use a competitor's power factor to calculate scored points. Targets are divided into three different scoring zones—A, C, and D. Competitors are awarded more points when shooting major power factor across the lower-scoring C and D zones. Competitors are awarded the same points for A-zone hits, regardless of major or minor power factor.

Hit Factor

Hit factor is a way to measure a competitor's ability to score points, without penalties, in the shortest amount of time. The scoring objective in competition is to get the highest hit factor you can across all stages in a match. Hit factor stage score is calculated by totaling your scored hits, minus any penalties, and dividing by the time needed to complete the stage.

Stage Points

Stage points are awarded to competitors based on their relative performance to each other. Each stage will have a maximum stage point value based on the number of rounds needed to complete it. The highest hit factor on a stage receives 100% of the available stage points. Each remaining competitor's hit factor is compared to the stage winner to determine their percentage of awarded stage points.

Match Points

Match points represent the competitor's overall performance across all stages in a single contest and are the total of all awarded stage points. The competitor with the highest total match points is the winner. Matches are a great way to test your skill at speed and see how other competitors solve stages based on their skills and ideas.

How long is a match?

Match lengths will vary based on the number of stages and people competing. In a local match, you might shoot four to eight stages. Depending on the number of people in your squad, it may take your squad forty minutes to complete a stage. For example, if you have six stages, and each squad takes forty minutes to complete, this equates to four hours. It is recommended that you watch a local match to see how it works before you compete.

How do I see my results?

Most events are scored and managed through a software platform called PractiScore. This can be found at the following website: https://practiscore.com. Many clubs ask competitors to sign up online before a match. After the event, you can log in to determine your results for each stage and each division. You can also see your overall match score.

Rules

As in any formalized competition, there are rules. USPSA rules are designed to keep competitors and spectators safe so they can enjoy all the aspects of the sport. It is essential that you become familiar with the official USPSA rules. They can be found on the USPSA website at https://uspsa.org/rules.

CHAPTER 49
DIVISIONS AND CATEGORIES

USPSA divisions recognize groupings of different handgun equipment and platforms and allow contestants to compete using equipment with similar capabilities. Categories are individual segments within a division that recognize groups of competitors. Match scores are separated by division and category to recognize performance within each group.

DIVISIONS

All competitors must declare and comply with the rules for a given division before engaging in a competition. The overviews that follow should help you quickly understand at a high level what each USPSA division is about, but please note that this is not a substitution for a competitor's understanding of the official rules. It is your responsibility to check the official rules and understand them before you compete or make any modifications to your pistol. The official USPSA division rules can be found at https://uspsa.org.

OPEN

The Open division is made up of all-out race guns, highly customized to go fast. Open allows for the most modifications and has the least restrictions of any pistol division. Many are custom-built and designed just for USPSA competition.

Experimentation with equipment has always contributed to the success of USPSA, and Open division is where the newest equipment ideas get refined. Modifications include ported barrels, compensators, optics, electronic sights, large-capacity magazines, special holsters, and magazine pouches, with no restrictions around pistol size or weight. The Open division supports major and minor power factor scoring.

Example - Open Division

Popular calibers: .38 Super, .38 Super Comp, 9mm+, .40 S&W and some .45 ACP. The .38 Super and 9mm+ are the most popular, as they can make major power factor with more rounds per magazine. Rimfire pistols are not allowed.

The Open division is not the best place for new shooters to start in the sport, but it is a lot of fun to watch competitors shoot these types of firearms in competition. Open is the most relaxed division when it comes to modifications, but these types of guns tend to be expensive and require high-pressure, tuned ammunition in order to perform reliably.

Open division pistols may use magazines up to 171.25mm (sometimes referred to as just 170mm).

LIMITED

The Limited division is one of the most popular USPSA divisions. It is made up of semi-automatic pistols with higher capacity magazines, iron sights, and major or minor power factor scoring. It typically has a large number of competitors.

This division allows for more customization than the Production division but not to the extremes of the Open division. The higher capacity magazines give you more options when shooting a stage and allow you to focus on shooting at speed instead of always having to reload.

Example - Limited Division

Supported modifications include enhanced grips, grip tape, expanded magazine wells, magazine releases, magazine and base plates, barrel replacements, trigger upgrades, guide rods, springs, and sights. It also supports fine-tuning of any internal parts of the gun.

You cannot use pistols with electronic sighting systems, compensators, or barrel porting. Limited lets you use special race holsters and magazine pouches with no restrictions around the pistol's size or weight. Limited supports both major and minor power factor scoring.

Popular calibers: .40 S&W and .45 ACP for major, and 9mm for minor. .40 S&W and 9mm are the most popular. 9mm can be a great way to get started and learn the sport. The .40 S&W round is the most popular, as it affords the highest power factor scoring using the most rounds in a magazine. Rimfire pistols are not allowed. Limited division pistols may use double-stack magazines up to 141.25mm in length (sometimes referred to as just 140mm). Competitors may also use single-stack guns in this division with magazine lengths up to 171.25mm (also referred to as just 170mm).

This is a great division where new shooters can get started, as it has all the benefits of being able to use out-of-the-box equipment you may already own while also allowing you to customize things over time.

LIMITED 10

This division was created so competitors in states that have laws around magazine capacity limits can still compete using a Limited division platform. Limited 10 uses most of the same rules and pistols from the standard Limited division.

The differences in Limited 10 are that the "10" refers to the maximum number of rounds you are allowed per magazine after the start signal. The other difference is magazine length when using a Single Stack 1911-style pistol. Single Stack 1911s may use magazines up to 171.25mm (sometimes referred to as 170mm) to accommodate up to ten rounds. All other pistols may use magazines up to 141.25mm (also referred to as 140mm) to hold their ten rounds. Either way, the ten-round limit reduces the capacity advantage some pistol platforms have over other higher capacity ones and creates an interesting competitive division.

SINGLE STACK 1911

This division supports Single Stack 'John Browning' 1911-style pistols. These pistols are metal, use only iron sights, and can weigh up to forty-five ounces with an empty magazine. Competition firearms need to fit in a regulation-size box with an empty magazine inserted. Single Stack 1911 supports both major and minor power factor scoring. Division rules allow eight rounds for major power factor scoring and ten rounds for minor power factor scoring. All equipment is worn on the belt using a "non-race-type" holster. Due to the limited number of rounds in each magazine, you may need to run six or more magazines on your belt to complete longer stages.

Example - Single Stack 1911

Popular calibers: The original 1911 pistol designs used .45 ACP, but newer models support .45 ACP and other calibers, like 9mm, .38 Super, 10mm, and .40 S&W. Competitors use these popular rounds following the power factor limits of eight rounds for major and ten rounds for minor. Competitors' pistols, with an empty magazine inserted, must fit wholly inside the official USPSA box with internal measures of 8 15/16 by 6 by 1 5/8 inches.

Single Stack 1911-style pistols are iconic firearms that have stood the test of time. They have been in continual service and production for over a century. They are a lot of fun to shoot, and there are lots of manufacturers and updated models to choose from.

PRODUCTION

The Production division is designed for stock factory, off-the-shelf firearms in the most popular designs from major manufacturers, which are available from local gun dealers. The guns for this division must be reviewed and approved by the National Range Officer Institute (NROI), and the approved list of pistols can be found on the USPSA Production gun list at https://uspsa.org/productionlist.

Example - Production Division

There are over fifty firearm manufacturers on the approved list arranged by manufacturer, pistol name, and factory weight. Firearm manufacturers must have 2,000 or more units built and available to purchase in order to be considered for the approved list. Almost every pistol manufacturer has several models that qualify for this division. All firearms need to fit in a regulation-size box with an empty magazine inserted. The 9mm pistols are the most popular caliber, as Production division uses only minor power factor scoring. Competitors may use major power factor ammunition, but there is no competitive scoring advantage like there is in the Limited division.

Popular calibers: Most competitors use 9mm, and some use .40 S&W. (Large calibers are permitted but will be scored using minor power factor.) The Production and Carry Optics divisions are the only divisions that explicitly score all competitors using minor power factor.

Production division allows for a maximum number of fifteen rounds per magazine, so you may need a few more magazines to complete larger courses of fire. Competitors' pistols, with an empty magazine inserted, must fit wholly inside the official USPSA box with internal measures of 8 15/16 by 6 by 1 5/8 inches.

Minor modifications for this division are allowed. Competitors may upgrade sights, add grip tape, and tune internal components. The pistol should maintain the limits of its original factory weight listed on the USPSA Production gun list.

CARRY OPTICS

This division uses approved Production firearms with extended magazine capacities and slide-mounted red dot sights. Only stock firearms listed on the USPSA-approved Production pistol list are permitted. There is a single maximum weight limit for all pistols of fifty-nine ounces—that includes the optic and one empty magazine.

Example - Carry Optics

Some people have referred to Carry Optics as "Open light" or "a poor man's Open division." It is a great way to compete using an electronic red dot and a Production platform, without all the specialized equipment used in the Open division. The red dots allow competitors to maintain a consistent target focus and, as such, faster target acquisition. All Carry Optics-approved pistols must have their red dots mounted so they reciprocate with the slide.

Popular calibers: This division uses only minor power factor scoring, so 9mm is the most popular caliber. Other calibers used include 357, .38 Colt, .38 Special, .38 Super, .40 S&W, and .45 ACP. (Note that large calibers are permitted but will be scored using minor power factor.) The Carry Optics and Production divisions are the only divisions that explicitly score all competitors using minor power factor.

Competitors may add grip tape or stippling, and they may tune internal components on the firearm. There is no stated limit to the number of rounds per magazine, but you will need to ensure your magazines and base pads fit in the official measuring tool (141.25mm).

REVOLVER

This division refers to double-action revolvers that have a minimum caliber requirement of .38/9mm. Competitors can choose major or minor power factor ammunition but will only be allowed six for major and eight for minor before having to reload. This division has no weight or size restrictions, barrel length, or minimum trigger pull—however, all pistols must use iron sights.

Example - Revolver

Popular calibers: The Revolver division includes .357, 9mm, .38 Colt, .38 Special, .38 Super, .40 S&W, and .45 ACP. Many competitors reload ammunition in this division, tuning their loads to hit the desired power factor and minimize recoil.

Modifications should be limited to improving cylinders, cylinder releases, tuning actions, upgrading sights, and changing grips. Competitors may use racing-style holsters, moon clips, and speed loaders that can be worn anywhere on the belt. Barrel porting and compensators are not permitted.

PCC

This division is one of the newer divisions in the USPSA competition. Pistol Caliber Carbine (PCC) is interesting in that it allows competitors to shoot what has traditionally been a pistol-only competition with pistol-caliber rifles. Because these firearms use pistol cartridges, they can shoot steel at closer ranges than traditional carbine rifles. Bullets need to be traveling at 1,600 FPS or less in competition to ensure safe firing distances on steel targets.

Example - Pistol Caliber Carbine

Popular calibers: The PCC division includes 9mm, .357 Sig, .40 S&W, 10mm, and .45 ACP. The 9mm can be a more popular round, as USPSA rules specify all scoring is minor power factor (125). Rimfire rifles are not allowed.

All rifles need an attached shoulder stock so they can be fired from a shouldered position. There is no limit on magazine capacity. The division allows rifles to compete with optics, iron sights, and slings. Firearms may be configured with compensators, muzzle brakes, or flash hiders, but no suppressors. There are a lot of new developments in PCC, and many competitors build their own rifles using different manufacturers' components to customize and gain an edge.

CATEGORIES

Categories are individual segments within a division that recognize specific groups of competitors. They are ideal for larger competitions where you have more than two or three people registered in an individual category.

USPSA recognizes the following categories:

- Lady – Female gender as listed on a government-issued ID.
- Junior – Competitors under the age of eighteen on the first day of the match.
- Senior – Competitors over the age of fifty-five on the first day of the match.
- Super Senior – Competitors over the age of sixty-five on the first day of competition.
- Military – Military personnel on current active-duty orders.
- Law Enforcement – Full-time law enforcement officers.

CHAPTER 50
TARGETS AND POWER FACTOR

TARGETS

USPSA competitions support nine different official scoring targets. These are divided into two types of cardboard targets and seven kinds of steel targets. Competitive stages may be built using any combination of the official targets.

Cardboard Targets

The two types of cardboard targets are the USPSA and the IPSC. The USPSA cardboard target is the most common and was formerly called a metric target. The IPSC target is slightly smaller and was formerly referred to as a classic target. The new naming convention helps distinguish primary usage for each target even though both are used in USPSA competitions.

Each target is made from corrugated cardboard and comes with pre-stamped or outlined scoring areas. These are labeled in order of zones (e.g., A, C, and D). *Note: Some older USPSA targets may have an additional zone B marking. This is because the scoring rules were simplified in 2019, and as a result, the B scoring zone was removed. This area is now scored as a C zone.*

Cardboard targets are designed to measure your accuracy. You get more points for achieving a center target A-zone hit than you would for a C- or D-zone hit.

All cardboard targets score up to five points per A-zone hit. Most stages specify two scoring hits per target for a maximum of ten points. Some standards or classifier stages can specify more than two hits, but it must be called out in the written stage brief.

USPSA Target

The overall full-size dimensions are 29.53 inches high and 17.72 inches wide. The center mass A zone is 11.02 by 5.91 inches.

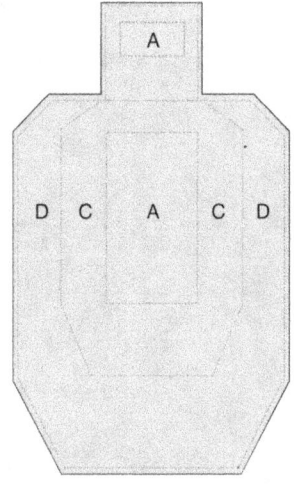

USPSA Target

IPSC Target

The overall full-size dimensions are 22.44 inches high and 17.72 inches wide. The center mass A zone is 12.8 inches high, and tapers at the top and bottom.

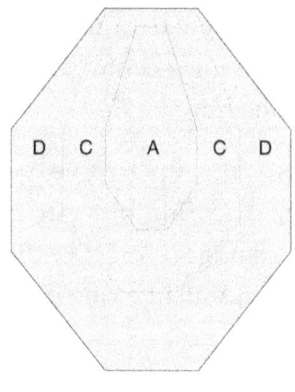

IPSC Target

Steel Targets

As mentioned above, steel targets are not scored for accuracy, but each one must fall on impact to score. A steel target is worth five points. There are five types of poppers and two kinds of knock-over plates.

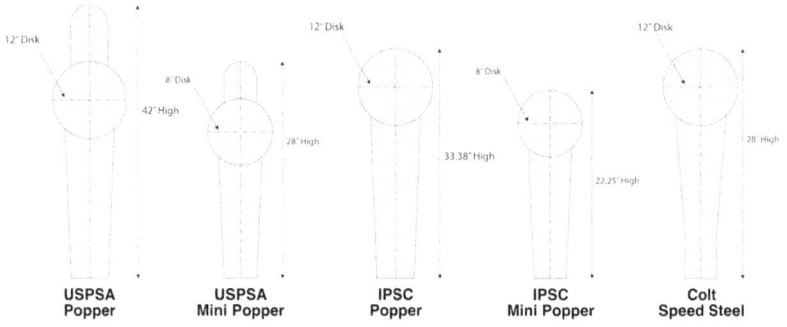

Steel Popper Targets

- **USPSA Popper** - The USPSA popper stands at 42 inches tall and has a 12-inch round circle.
- **USPSA Mini-Popper** - The USPSA mini-popper stands at 28 inches tall and has an 8-inch round circle.
- **IPSC Popper** - The IPSC popper stands at 33.37 inches tall and has a 12-inch round circle.

- **IPSC Mini-Popper** - The IPSC mini-popper is 22.5 inches tall and has an 8-inch round circle.
- **Colt Speed Steel** - The colt speed steel target is 28 inches tall and has a 12-inch round circle.

Knock-Over Plates

Metals plates are designed to fall over after being hit. These plates may be attached to a hinge to hold them in place. Round metal plates come in eight- and twelve-inch versions. Square or rectangular plates are six and twelve inches on each side.

Penalty Targets

Many courses of fire will incorporate penalty targets that raise the difficulty of individual shots on scoring targets. Penalty targets decrease the size of the scoring zone and provide a better challenge than just shooting at regular targets. Penalty targets also subtract from your score with each hit, so it is essential to understand how they impact your score.

No-Shoots

A no-shoot is a target that, when hit, generates a ten-point penalty toward your overall stage score. That means for every no-shoot you hit, you lose ten points on the stage, and there is no way to make up those points.

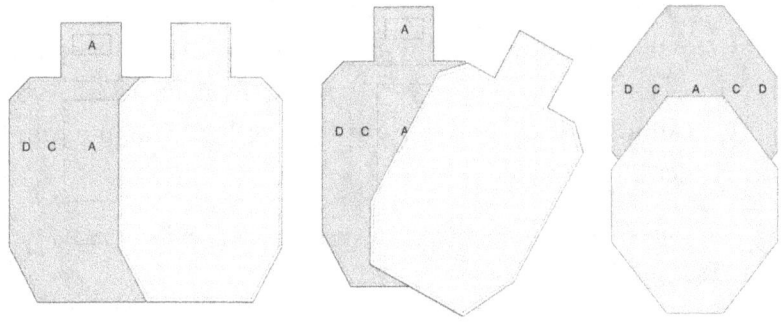

No-Shoot Examples

Hard-Cover Targets

A hard-cover target is used to decrease the size of scoring targets and is defined as solid or impenetrable in the rules. Hits on hard covers do not score points, but you don't lose any points either. You are able to get a full score by taking makeup shots where the stage rules do not limit the total number of shots.

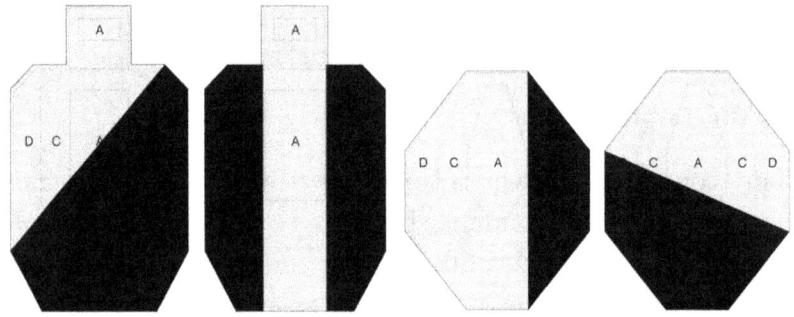

Hard-Cover Examples

POWER FACTOR

Power factor was designed to help keep the playing field equal for competitors around ammunition performance and recoil. Power factor calculation is a way to measure the relative performance of a competitor's ammunition in their firearm.

When your pistol generates lower recoil or muzzle flip, your ability to take accurate follow-up shots and shoot faster on target are increased. When you have a heavier recoil, your ability to shoot quickly and accurately is reduced, as the gun is more difficult to control.

(See the chapter on chronographs for measuring a bullet's velocity in feet per second.)

• • •

Major vs. Minor

Power factors are grouped into two types—major and minor. Minor power factor will have a rating of 125 to 164, and major is 165 or higher.

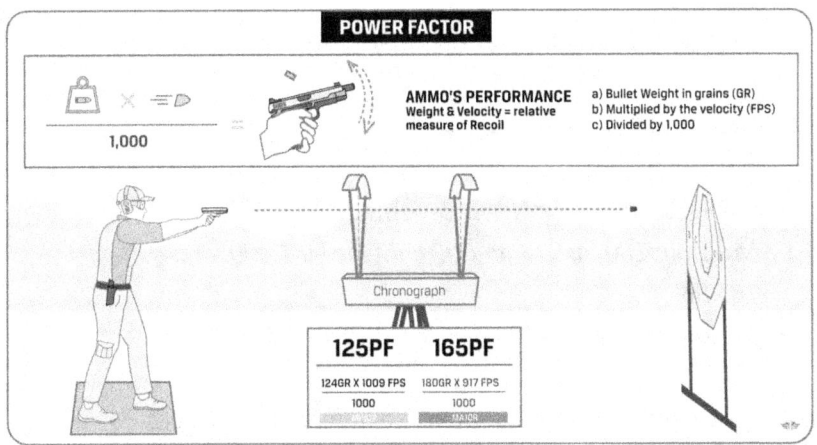

Major vs. Minor Power Factor

Larger calibers and cartridges are more commonly used to make major power factor, because they support larger powder loads. Smaller centerfire cartridges, like 9mm, are more common in minor.

Calculating Power Factor

The power factor calculation uses your bullet's weight in grains, multiplies that by the velocity in feet per second, then divides it by 1,000. For example: [Bullet Weight (Grains) x Velocity (Feet Per Second)] / 1,000 = Power Factor (PF).

- Minor PF = 125 to 164
- Major PF = 165 or greater

Minor Power Factor Example:

- 9mm 124 GR bullet traveling at 1,009 Feet Per Second (FPS).
- *Multiply 124 by 1,009 and then divide by 1,000, and you get 125.116.*
- Minor 125 PF = (124 GR x 1009 FPS) / 1,000.

Major Power Factor Example:

- .40 S&W 180 GR bullet traveling at 917 FPS.
- *Multiply 180 by 917 and then divide by 1,000, and you get 165.06.*
- Major 165 PF = (180 GR x 917 FPS) / 1,000.

Note: Any ammunition and pistol combination that does not perform at or above the minor 125 PF floor cannot receive a stage or match score.

Power Factor Hits

Ammunition performance affects how you score cardboard targets. Major power factor is awarded more points for less accurate hits on cardboard targets. This difference may not seem like much on a single target, until it is taken across an entire stage of multiple targets.

Zone	Major PF (165)	Minor PF (125)
A	5 Points	5 Points
C	4 Points	3 Points
D	2 Points	1 Points

Minor Power Factor has the same hit score when shooting A (alpha) zone hits. Minor is awarded fewer points across other scoring zones because of the lighter recoil.	**Major Power Factor** has a higher overall hit score across target zones because it is deemed harder to control recoil and get back on target.
All ammunition must perform at, or above, the designated floor of 125 PF in USPSA competition. The most popular minor power factor ammunition is 9mm.	All ammunition eligible for major power factor scoring must perform at or above the 165 PF floor, to count for major scoring. Popular major power factor ammunition is 38 Super, .40S&W and 45 ACP.

Major vs. Minor Hits

When shooting anything other than alphas, the differences in major and minor hit scoring start to appear. This example shows two hits: one alpha and one charlie. Depending on the power factor (PF), different points will be awarded.

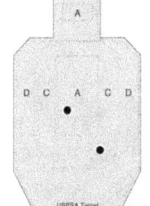

Scoring Zone	Major	Minor
A	5	5
C	4	3
Total	9	8

Major vs. Minor scoring

Major will get five for the A and four for the C, for a total of nine points. Minor will get the same five for the A but will get only three points for the C, for a total of eight points.

If you are competing in a single power factor division, you won't need to think about the differences in multiple power factor scoring. However, if you are shooting with minor power factor and your competitors are shooting major, it is important to understand the examples below to play a competitive game.

When you shoot minor power factor in a USPSA division that supports major and minor, you must understand how the lower recoil contributes to your performance and if it is worth it. There is a progressive decrease in target scores as you move from all alphas to a mix of other scoring zones.

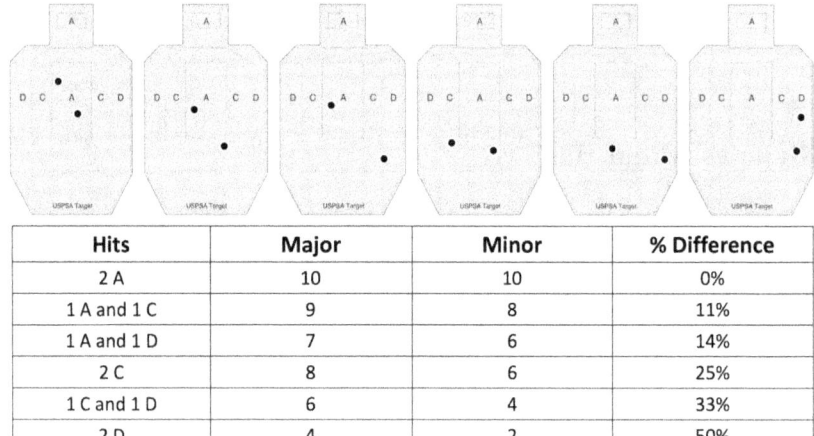

Hits	Major	Minor	% Difference
2 A	10	10	0%
1 A and 1 C	9	8	11%
1 A and 1 D	7	6	14%
2 C	8	6	25%
1 C and 1 D	6	4	33%
2 D	4	2	50%

Major vs Minor scoring percentages

For Open, Limited, Limited 10, Single Stack 1911, and Revolver divisions, you will collect higher points using major power factor ammunition. For divisions like Production and Carry Optics, everyone is scored using minor power factor only, so there is no advantage to shooting major.

CHAPTER 51
COURSE TYPES AND MATCH LEVELS

COURSE TYPES

Course types help course designers create stages that test competitors' skills across a wide range of challenges.

Short Courses:

These courses accommodate up to two shooting locations and require no more than twelve rounds to complete. The stage design should not allow you to shoot the entire stage from any single location or view of the targets. Short course designs should not let you shoot more than eight scoring hits from one location or view.

In summary, short courses offer:

- Maximum number of shooting locations: up to two.
- Maximum scoring hits per location or view: up to eight.
- Number of rounds needed to complete: up to twelve.
- Maximum points: 12 hits x 5 points = 60.
- Scoring rules: Comstock, Virginia Count, or Fixed.

Medium Courses:

These are designed to accommodate up to three shooting locations and require no more than twenty rounds to complete. Medium course designs should not allow you to shoot and score more than eight hits from one location or view of the targets. These courses can incorporate props or require a demonstration of dominant- and supporting-hand shooting skills.

In summary, medium courses offer:

- Maximum number of shooting locations: up to three.
- Maximum scoring hits per location or view: up to eight.
- Number of rounds needed to complete: thirteen to twenty.
- Maximum points: 20 hits x 5 points = 100.
- Scoring rules: Comstock.

Long Courses:

Long courses have no limit on the number of shooting locations and can encompass up to thirty-two rounds. You can only shoot and score up to eight hits from one location or view of the targets. These courses can incorporate props or require a demonstration of dominant- and supporting-hand shooting skills.

In summary, long courses offer:

- Maximum number of shooting locations: no limit.
- Maximum scoring hits per location or view: up to eight.
- Number of rounds needed to complete: twenty-one to thirty-two.
- Maximum points: 32 hits x 5 points = 160.
- Scoring rules: Comstock.

Location vs. Views

Locations are defined as physical spaces within the boundaries of the course of fire. A change in location occurs when both feet have moved to a new physical position where additional targets can be engaged.

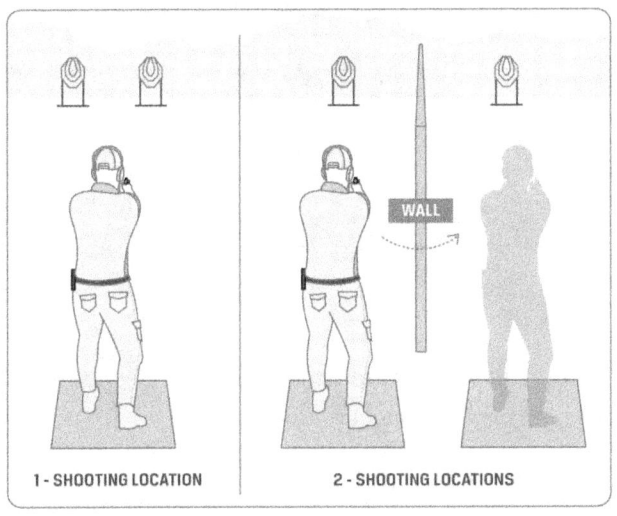

Locations

One Location - Two targets are engaged from one location because you are not required to move your feet to a new position to take the targets.

Two Locations - Two targets engaged from two locations because you are required to move your feet to a new position to take the targets.

Views are specific to what you can see when you are looking at an array of targets. Vision barriers and walls are used to create multiple views from a single location. However, *one location may offer multiple views.*

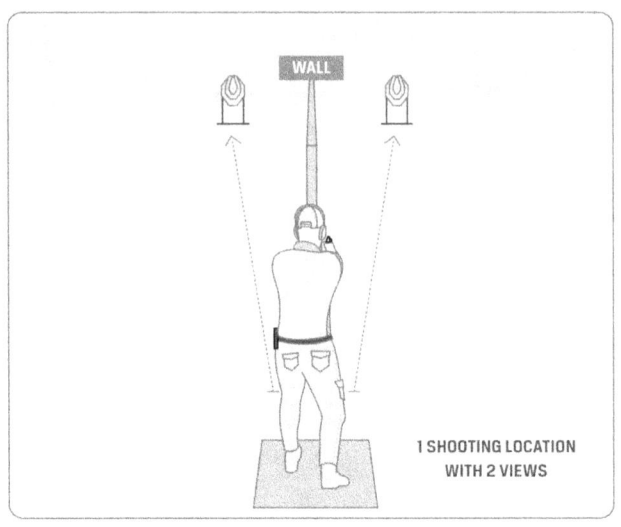

Views

In competition, competitors are required to move across multiple locations and change views to engage all targets.

Special and Supplemental Courses

Special course types are used to design stages that test specific skills and create consistent courses of fire that can be set up, shot, and scored consistently for competition and classification.

Standards - Standards are two or more separately timed strings totaled together to produce a final stage score. Standards can be up to twenty-four rounds or less and scored under the Virginia Count or Fixed Time scoring systems. Standard stages use only cardboard targets and may require specific skills to be demonstrated on the clock. Standards courses may require specific shooting positions across multiple locations, mandatory reloads, and dominant-, supportive-hand shooting.

Speed Shoot - Speed shoots are completed in one continuous string of fire of sixteen rounds or less, from a single location in any order. Scoring is calculated under the Comstock or

Virginia Count rules. One mandatory reload may be required, and stage rules may specify which hand you shoot from after the reload.

Classifiers - A classifier is a specific stage or course of fire that is designed to measure a competitor's speed and accuracy within a division. Classifiers may require mandatory reloads, specific shooting positions, specific shooting locations, and a demonstration of dominant- or support-hand shooting. All USPSA classifiers follow a published set of rules with notes and diagrams. The classifier documentation outlines everything needed to set up, shoot, and score the stage consistently. Hit factor scores for classifiers are recorded nationwide and loaded into a scoring database to facilitate the USPSA classification ranking. Details on the most current USPSA Classifiers can be found at https:// uspsa.org.

Shoot-Off - Shoot-offs are supplementary courses of fire where competitors shoot directly against each other on a simultaneous stage using similar but individual targets. Shoot-off stages are usually a maximum of nine rounds and will require one mandatory reload. These courses are similar to drag races as competitors compete head to head for the best times.

MATCH LEVELS

Match Levels help set expectations for USPSA organizers and competitors around frequency, rules, and governance.

Level 1: Club matches - USPSA local clubs run monthly or bi-monthly events throughout the year. Local competitions are ideal, as you will not only have the opportunity to practice, but you will also learn how to play the game.

Level 2: Sectional or State matches - These are open to participants from different clubs and held on an annual basis.

Sectionals and state competitions attract the top shooters in their area.

Level 3: Annual championship matches by area or region - USPSA areas are groupings of states near one another. There are eight area groupings across the United States. Area events are a great way to see the best competitors in your region and visit other clubs' locations.

Nationals – USPSA Annual Championships - National Championships are where the best of the best go to compete every year. These events are hosted at large venues and governed by USPSA. The competitions are organized around USPSA divisions requiring contestants to compete with the same type of equipment. These events draw hundreds of competitors to compete for the national title within each division.

For more information on local clubs and matches, go to https://uspsa.org/matches or https://practiscore.com.

You don't need to be a USPSA member to compete in Level 1 matches. However, after competing in a few matches, you will most likely want to join USPSA so you can track your performance and progress.

CHAPTER 52
WRITTEN STAGE BRIEFINGS AND DIAGRAMS

WRITTEN STAGE BRIEFINGS (WSB)

Written stage briefings (or WSBs) are the official plans of all match stages and are used to present consistent information about the stage to all competitors before they compete. Written stage briefings are approved by the range master and are posted at each stage before the match begins.

The range officer in charge of the squad or stage must read the WSB aloud exactly as it is written at the start of each stage briefing. The WSB will describe how competitors should engage at the starting position, how the stage will be scored using Comstock, Virginia Count, or Fixed Time rules, and the number of target types. It also covers the number of rounds needed for a perfect score, and the number of total points available. Moving targets will be activated by the RO so everyone can see the movement and timing of the target prior to competing. After the stage briefing, competitors are allowed to walk through and inspect the course of fire. *Note: The RO may specify a time limit for walk-throughs to keep things moving.*

Changes - When there are changes to a stage layout, stage diagrams may not always be updated—but changes that impact the written stage briefings must be updated and covered during the stage briefing. The WSB overrides any other type of communication and is therefore considered the most up-to-date source of information.

Stage Brief Outline - The rules around the stage brief outline can be found on the USPSA website under "Handgun Competition Rules" and can include the following:

- Scoring methods
- Targets
- Number of rounds (minimums)
- Firearm ready and starting positions
- Start/stop signals (visual or audible)
- Stage procedures

Stage Diagrams

Stage diagrams are a great way to get an overview of a stage layout and enable competitors to start visualizing a stage. The diagrams can show target position, target names, shooting areas, and a starting position. The visual diagram helps staff and competitors understand the design layout described in the WSB.

Setup Notes

Setup notes are often included with stage diagrams. They cover additional detail around how a stage is configured and can specify target heights, distances, types, shooting box sizes, etc., to ensure stage consistency.

CHAPTER 53
CHRONOGRAPHS AND AMMO TESTING

Chronographs are instruments that measure time. In USPSA, they are used to measure the velocity of ammunition fired from a gun. The velocity of the bullet and its weight are used to calculate power factor. Chronographs measure a bullet's speed by timing how long it takes a projectile to pass over two sensors. The sensors trigger a clock that records the time and then calculates the velocity in feet per second.

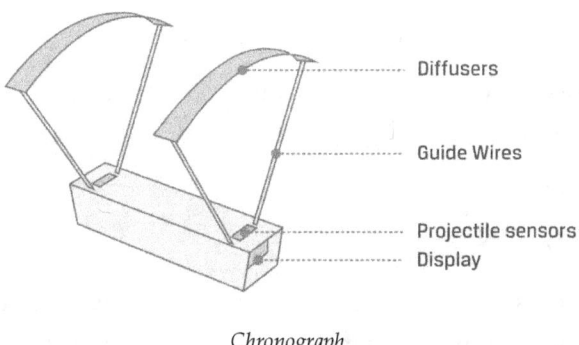

Chronograph

It is important to check the chronograph's manual for the required distance from the device before you begin testing.

Ensure your shots travel between the measuring area of the device so you get good samples. It is recommended that you set up a target on the other side of the chronograph to help track your aim. You don't want to accidentally shoot your chronograph. Use a bench rest if it helps steady your aim and take time to ensure a clean shot.

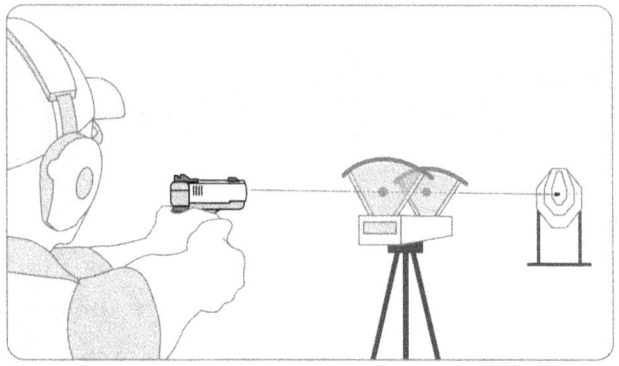

Velocity Test

When a bullet travels through the measuring area, you will get a 'feet per second' reading (or FPS). Power factor is then calculated by taking the weight of the bullet, multiplying it by the velocity, and then dividing by 1,000.

Power Factor (PF) = (Weight x Velocity) / 1,000

For example, if you are using a 147-grain bullet which travels at 860 FPS, the power factor would be: (147 GR x 860 FPS) / 1,000 = 136.42 PF.

AMMO TESTING

Eight samples are drawn, and the competitor will be required to demonstrate a power factor using their firearm at the appointed time. If a competitor fails to demonstrate their gun at the appointed time, they are disqualified and removed from the match results.

Usually, the chronograph station is an official stage in the match. You will want to follow *all* requests from the designated chrono officer (CRO) on this stage. The chrono officer will inspect each competitor's firearm to ensure compliance with your declared division. They will want to see that your gun is safe to operate and the safety mechanisms are in working order.

One of the eight ammo samples is used to measure the actual bullet's weight. At least three bullets are fired to measure velocity, and a maximum of six may be used to demonstrate the stated power factor.

Power Factor (PF) = [Bullet Weight (Grains) x Velocity (Feet Per Second)] / 1,000. Final results ignore decimal places.

- The minimum power factor for major is 165.
- The minimum power factor for minor is 125.

It is wise to dial in your reloads or check that your purchased ammo is above the PF floors to ensure performance at your desired level. If you are reloading your ammunition, you may target a higher floor to ensure a comfortable margin (170 for major and 130 for minor). The main thing is to know your ammunition and how it performs before you get to the chronograph station.

Reloads

When reloading ammunition, measure how fast and powerful your specific loads are in your firearm, as each gun causes ammunition to perform differently. As you start to dial in your reloading process, you will begin to understand what bullet weight, powder, and recipe you prefer to work with. You will experience more success when you can produce consistent velocity and power factors through your reloading process.

• • •

Scoring and Power Factor

If a power factor test fails to meet the major floor, the competitor's PF will be evaluated to see if it meets the minor floor. If minor is met, then the match scores will be calculated or recalculated using minor. If minor is *not* met, then the competitor may be allowed to shoot the match without any match recognition or awarding an actual score.

CHAPTER 54
TARGET SCORING AND PENALTIES

Best Hits on Cardboard Score

When scoring cardboard targets, only your best two hits on the target are scored. This means the maximum value per cardboard target is ten points. The only time this is different is on courses where it is specified in the written stage brief (WSB).

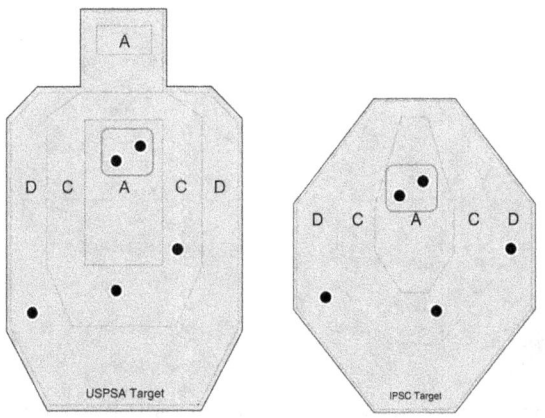

Best hits count for score

In this example, you can see more than two shots on a single target, but only the best two hits will count toward the target score. In this example, the maximum value per target is ten points, and as the best two shots are A-zone hits, five points each, so ten points are awarded. The extra shots do not count toward the target score; however, all of the time used to take the extra shots will count toward your stage score. Therefore, you need to have a balance between your speed and accuracy to achieve the best match score.

Steel Targets

Steel targets come in several sizes and should be calibrated to fall when you hit the center of the target. There is no difference when scoring steel targets using major or minor power factor. Steel targets score just like A zone hits after they have been knocked over—they are worth five points each, regardless of shape or size. A steel target is considered a reactive target, so the steel must fall to score.

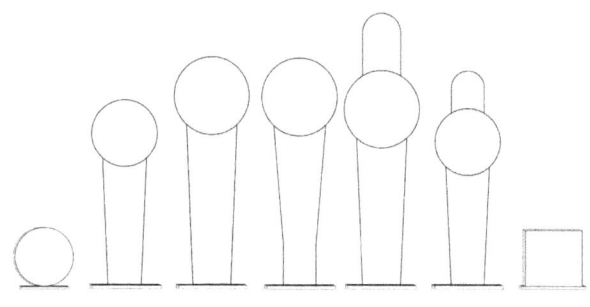

USPSA Steel Targets

PENALTIES

Penalties on targets are driven from two types: the mike (or the missing shot) and the "no-shoot." Each one carries a penalty of ten points. When stages are designed, targets may be surrounded by no-shoot or hard-cover areas. These designs limit the scoring target area on a target, increasing the difficulty of shots and raising the incentive for accuracy.

Miss (mikes) - Mikes occur when there are less than the number of required hits on a scoring target. For example, the scoring target requires two hits, but only hit was recorded.

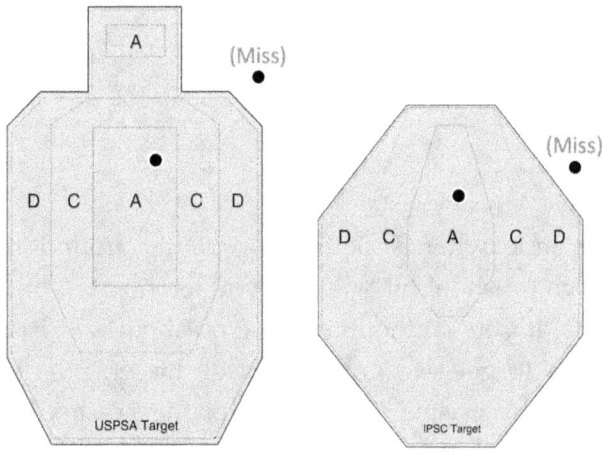

Missing hits on target

The missing hit on the target would be assessed as a mike penalty. Each missing hit on the scoring target reduces your score by ten points.

No-Shoot (NS) - No-shoot penalties occur when you accidentally hit or shoot a white target. No-shoots are standard cardboard targets turned around backward, so the white side is facing the competitor. They are usually stapled over standard cardboard targets to decrease the size of the scoreable shooting area.

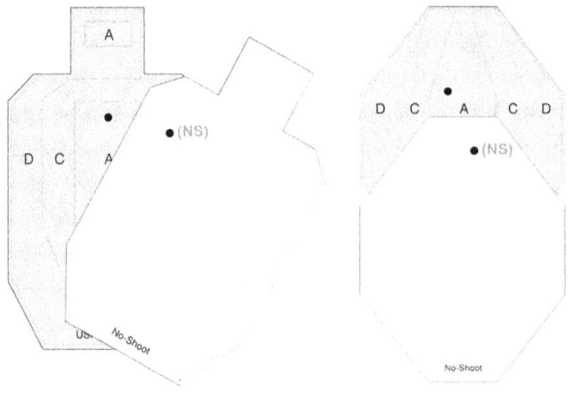
No-Shoot

Take your time when shooting for points around no-shoots, because each no-shoot hit will cost you ten points—or two good scoring hits. If you do the math, one no-shoot will cost you the time it takes to get two good shots on target, plus the points earned, plus the wasted time taken for the no-shoot. You can't make up those points, so you want to avoid hitting the no-shoot as much as possible.

Note: Some no-shoot targets can have an "X" across the target. Both are valid no-shoot targets in competition.

Procedural - Procedural penalties are usually just mistakes or mental errors, so it helps to understand how to run a clean stage and avoid them.

A common procedural penalty is where you fail to follow the course description or written stage brief. As an example, this includes:

- Shooting at, or engaging, a target with one foot outside the designated shooting area or over a fault line.
- Forgetting to do something specified in the written stage brief, such as a mandatory reload.
- Shooting more shots than specified.

- Failing to shoot at a scoring target.
- Failing to engage with the designated dominant or supportive hand.

Each occurrence of a procedural will deduct ten points, and some can be assessed per shot. The most common procedural penalty is engaging a target from outside the designated shooting area. These points can add up fast, so it is good to understand the course description before you start your run.

Hard Cover and Soft Cover

Hard-Cover Targets

Hard-cover targets have black areas that are used to decrease the size of the scoring zone and increase difficulty. Hits on hard-cover targets do not score points, but you don't lose any points either.

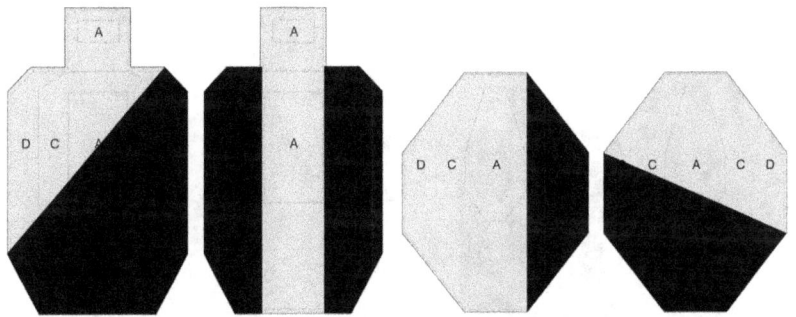

Hard-Cover target examples

Hard-Cover Barriers

Barriers are used to create the stage environment and give competitors a playing field for competition. Hard-cover barriers should be considered as solid planes that reach from the ground to the sky unless otherwise designated in stage briefs and diagrams. Examples of hard-cover barriers are barrels, vision screens, and walls. It is important to note that any bullets passing through hard-cover barriers and striking scoring targets do not count for score.

Soft-Cover Barriers

Soft-cover barriers look very similar to hard-cover barriers. They are similarly used to obscure scoring target areas. However, when your bullet passes through a soft cover and strikes a scoring target, it scores, and if it hits a penalty target, you are penalized. Soft-cover targets are used to obscure targets to add interest to stage design.

Hard-Cover Target Scoring Examples

Example 1

This example illustrates two cardboard targets, T1 and T2. The T2 target has hard cover, reducing the available scoring area. The competitor is shooting major power factor.

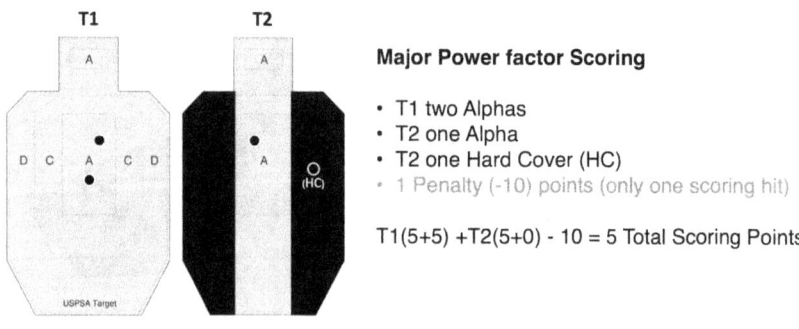

Scoring Example 1

T1 gets two alphas, and T2 receives two shots, one alpha and one in the hard cover (HC). Because there is only one scoring hit on T2, a miss (M) penalty is assessed at negative ten points. (Remember, hits on hard-cover targets do not score points, but you don't lose any points either.) Each missing hit is ten penalty points.

T1(5 + 5) + T2(5 + 0) − 10 = 5 Total Scoring Points

Example 2:

This example illustrates two cardboard targets, T1 and T2. The T2 target has a hard cover, reducing the available scoring area—just like the first example. The competitor is shooting major power factor.

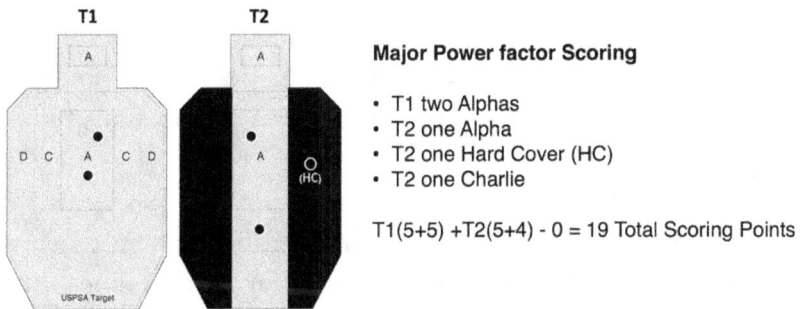

Scoring Example 2

T1 gets two alphas, and T2 receives three shots: one alpha, one hard cover, and one charlie.

The hard-cover hit does not count for score and does not incur a penalty. There are two scoring hits on T2, so therefore there are no missing shots. This example illustrates how the best available scoring hits per target count.

T1(5 + 5) + T2(5 + 4) − 0 = 19 Total Scoring Points

Note: When stage rules don't limit the total number of shots, quick makeup shots are a good way to reduce missing shot penalties.

• • •

Target Scoring Lines

USPSA cardboard targets have scoring zones stamped on them that make evaluating alpha, charlie, and delta hits straightforward. The targets incorporate scoring lines that provide a consistent method of evaluating shots that directly hit or span multiple scoring zones and penalty areas.

Each bullet, as it passes through a target, will create a hole with a grease ring. The hole will contract slightly after the round passes, but the grease ring remains and should be used to assess shots that are close to, or in contact with, a scoring line.

Competitors receive the higher point values of adjacent scoring areas when the bullet hole or grease ring touches a scoring line. Competitors may also be assessed penalties when holes or grease rings clip the edges of perforations on no-shoot targets.

Scoring Overlay

Scoring overlays are used to evaluate cardboard targets when the bullet holes are too close to scoring or penalty lines. The scoring overlay is made up of lines and five circles that cover the different bullet calibers used in USPSA competition.

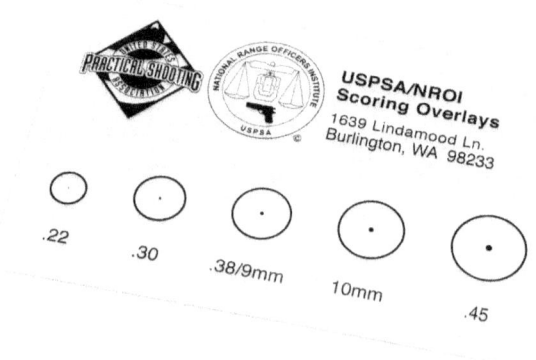

USPSA Scoring Overlay

The cards have bullet calibers from .22/5.56mm, 30/7.62mm, .38/9mm, .40/10mm, and .45/11.43mm. The overlay tool and methods provide a consistent way to review shots on targets by different bullet calibers.

How to Use an Overlay

The first step when using the overlay card is to determine what caliber the competitor is shooting with, so you use the correct bullet outline on the overlay. Cardboard holes contract after a bullet passes through, so the grease ring will appear slightly smaller than the size of the original bullet.

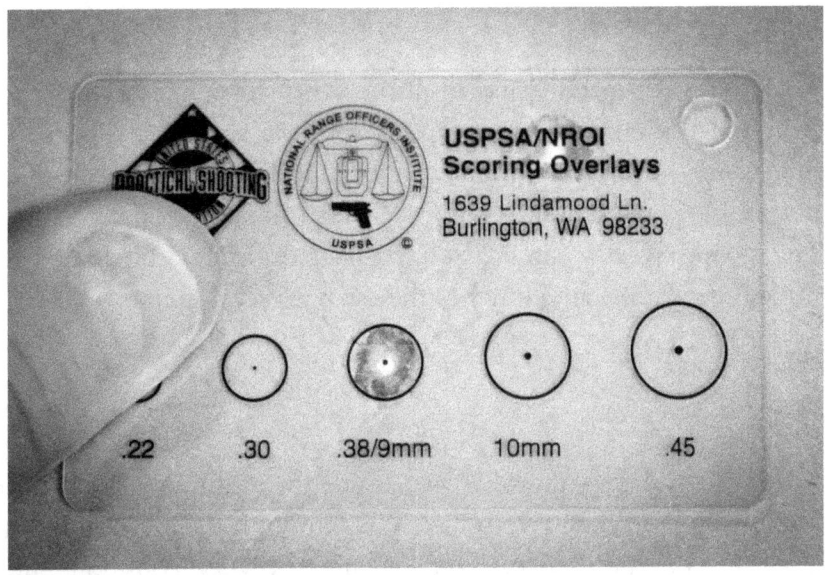

USPSA Scoring Overlay on Target

To check a target, you center the correct caliber circle over the center of the bullet hole's grease ring.

Note: Use the grease ring to help you center the overlay ring on the bullet hole (overlay templates have dots in the center of each hole to help you line things up). It is also important to use the transparent template when evaluating scoring hits, as it does not change or damage a target after it has been shot. Don't push bullet holes in from the back side of the target to score them. This will distort the grease ring size, making it harder to determine the actual score.

Review what you see. Is the outside diameter of the overlay circle touching a scoring line or dividing an adjacent scoring or penalty area? Any hits touching the higher scoring zone on a target receive the higher scoring value.

Overlays can be used to assess penalties when shots are on or near non-scoring targets. If you have a no-shoot and the bullet hole clips the edge of the white cardboard, you can check to see if the grease ring touches the perforation. If it does, the penalty is assessed.

Sometimes you need to use multiple overlays to connect scoring lines when there is a lot of tape covering a scoring perforation line. One overlay is used to connect the line from one visible perforation to another, creating a clear visual of the scoring line. The second overlay can be used to assess the bullet hole to determine if the grease ring touches the overlaid scoring line.

Doubles

Scoring overlays can also be used to evaluate "doubles." Doubles occur when two bullets pass through the same hole, or close to the same hole. Doubles are not very common and become apparent when viewed through an overlay.

Doubles are not awarded automatically if there is only one hole visible on a target. Two overlays will be used to carefully inspect for two grease rings close, but slightly off-center, from one another. If there is no visible evidence of two scoring hits on the cardboard, only one scoring hit may be counted.

· · ·

Example 1

Hits touching a scoring line between two scoring zones get the benefit of the higher scoring zone's value.

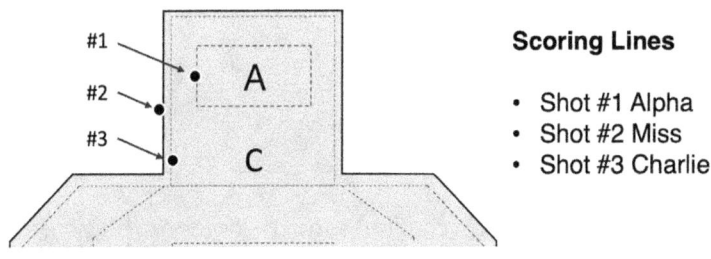

Scoring Lines - Example 1

The first hit breaks the scoring perforation of the A zone and would be scored an A (alpha). The second hit breaks the edge of the cardboard but does not break the C-zone scoring perforation, so it would be scored a miss. The third hit breaks the scoring perforation of the C zone and would be scored C (charlie).

Minor scoring example - best two hits count for score:

1 A (alpha) +5 points

1 C (charlie) +3 points

Total of 8 points for this target using minor scoring.

Example 2

Hits touching a scoring line between scoring zones and a no-shoot receive the scoring area that is visible and a no-shoot penalty.

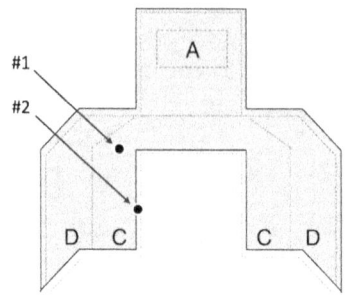

Scoring Lines

- Shot #1 Charlie
- Shot #2 Charlie + NS (no-shoot)

Scoring Lines - Example 2

The first hit scores a C (charlie), and the second hit scores a C (charlie) because it breaks the perforation to the C zone. The second hit also gets a NS (no-shoot) penalty because it breaks the perforation on the no-shoot.

Minor scoring example - all scoring hits + penalties:

1 C (charlie) +3 points

1 C (charlie) +3 points and 1 NS (no-shoot) penalty -10

Notice that shot number two does not get the higher A value behind the no-shoot because only the visible area of the scoring target may receive a score.

CHAPTER 55
STAGE SCORING AND RULES

HIT FACTOR

Hit factor is the measure of a competitor's performance and how well they can manage the balance of speed and accuracy. The number represents how many points you score per second on a given stage (i.e., the higher the number, the better your stage score).

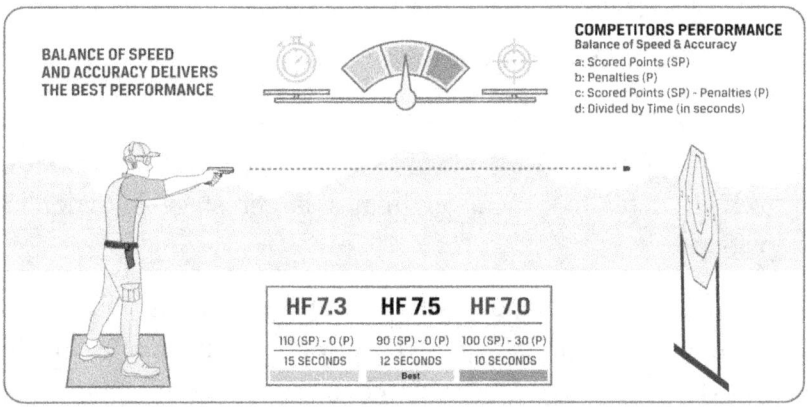

Hit Factor - Competitors Performance

Calculating Hit Factor

Your hit factor (HF) is calculated by adding your scored hits to get a total number of scored points (SP), minus any penalties (P), which gives you total points (TP) for the stage. You divide your total points by your stage time (T) to get your hit factor. The calculation looks like this: (scored points – penalties) / time = hit factor.

Hit Factor Examples

Notice that in all three of these examples below, the hit factors are very close, but it is the balance of speed and accuracy together that delivers the highest hit factor.

1. Most Penalties/Fastest Time

100 Scored Points (SP) with 30 Penalties (P) / 10 Seconds = **7.0 HF**

2. Highest Score/Slowest Time

110 Scored Points (SP) with 0 Penalties (P) / 15 Seconds = **7.3 HF**

3. Balance Speed and Accuracy Delivers the Highest HF

90 Scored Points (SP) with 0 Penalties (P) / 12 Seconds = **7.5 HF**

High Hit Factor vs. Low Hit Factor Stages

High hit factor (HF) stages are driven by higher points collected in a shorter period of time. Stages with fast transitions and low movement tend to run faster than a larger stage with longer transitions.

For example, say a stage has five cardboard targets, where two good hits on each target give you a total of fifty points for the stage. The stage has one quick change in view, but only one shooting location. You complete a perfect run in five seconds.

The hit factor would be 10. I.e., (50 points − 0 penalties) / 5.0 seconds = 10.

In this example, you averaged around ten scoring points per second, so your score adds up very fast.

Low hit factor (HF) stages collect fewer points over a longer period of time. Stages with longer transition times, high movement, and harder targets will take longer to collect the highest scoring points.

For example, let's take a similar stage example to the one above and increase the number of available scoring targets from five to fifteen. This means that there are three times more points available for a maximum of 150 points. If we introduce several transitions that add twenty-five seconds to the overall stage time, we get a new total of thirty seconds.

If all stage points (150), can be completed with the same accuracy in thirty seconds, then the hit factor is (150 points − 0 penalties) / 30 seconds equals a hit factor of 5.0.

In this example, you would have averaged around five scoring points per second. Even though there are more points available, it takes longer to get through fifteen targets and multiple transitions.

How to Improve Your Hit Factor

When you look at a stage, you should assess your ability to move efficiently through the course of fire in order to achieve the best score in the shortest amount of time. If you watch the top-ranking competitors, you will notice that all the little things add up to support scoring a higher hit factor.

For example, assess the way you enter a shooting position with your gun up, ready to engage—or how fast you can exit a position to get to the next one. The top competitors make the movements look effortless as they collect the highest points.

In summary, use the highest power factor for your division, get better scoring hits, watch your penalties, and operate quickly to achieve the highest hit factor. It takes a balance of all three to win.

STAGE SCORING RULES

There are three types of stage scoring rules applied to courses of fire. These include Comstock, Virginia Count, and Fixed Time. Each format has similar and unique combinations that create an exciting and competitive challenge.

Comstock

Comstock scoring rules are one of the most common stage rules used in USPSA competition. These rules have no restrictions on the time it takes to complete the course of fire, the number of shots fired, or the number of hits on a target.

Each target is scored using your best scoring hits up to a maximum number defined in the written stage brief. The most common maximum is two. If two hits are the maximum, then each cardboard target would be worth ten points.

You can shoot cardboard targets as much as you like under Comstock rules to ensure good scoring zone hits, but all the time taken will be factored into your overall hit factor score. The best hit factor scores are a balance of high-scoring hits in the shortest amount of time.

Hit Factor = Points Scored / Time

Target penalties under Comstock rules are assessed for procedurals, misses, and no-shoot hits. Penalty mikes and no-shoot hits incur a penalty of ten points for each occurrence. Just one of these penalties is the equivalent to two alpha-scoring shots. Missing scoring hits on targets is costly, because you don't get any points *and* you are assessed a penalty for each missing shot on a cardboard target.

Example - Missing Hit vs. Makeup Shot Under Comstock Rules

In the example below, we will use Comstock rules and minor power factor scoring. We will compare the overall hit factors between Example 1 where the competitor shoots one alpha and one mike vs. Example 2 where the competitor shoots one alpha, one mike, and one alpha makeup shot.

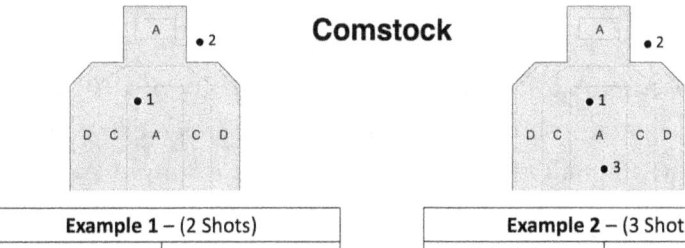

Comstock

Example 1 – (2 Shots)	
(A) Alpha	5
Penalties	-10
Score	-5
Time (seconds)	1.25
Hit Factor	0*

* Hit Factor cannot be negative

Example 2 – (3 Shots)	
(A) Alpha	10
Penalties	0
Score	10
Time (seconds)	2.0
Hit Factor	5

Example 1: There are two shots at the target, but only one hits and counts for a score, so a penalty miss is assessed for (-10) points. The miss in this example creates a deficit of (-5) points because two scoring hits are required, but when you add the missing hit penalty, it becomes even more expensive. (-5) + (-10) = 15 points in total penalties.

Example 2: There are two good-scoring hits on the target. The miss does not count, as there is no penalty for additional shots under Comstock rules. You could take multiple shots to improve your scoring hits, but you would be increasing your stage time. In this example, taking a quick third shot is better than a (-15) point penalty. It takes a little more time for the makeup shot, but the overall score and hit factor are improved.

VIRGINIA COUNT

Virginia Count scoring rules are more common in classifiers and standard stages. Virginia Count limits the number of rounds a competitor may shoot per target across the course of fire. There are no restrictions on the time it takes to complete the stage.

Virginia Count restricts the number of shots fired at a target and the number of hits per target. Best hits per scoring target count for your score. Additional shots incur a penalty of (-10) and are counted separately from extra hits on targets. One extra shot can get you two penalties if it hits a target. For example: extra shot (-10) + extra hit (-10) = 20 penalty points.

The big thing to remember under Virginia Count is taking enough time to get the scoring points you need without taking any extra shots.

Example - Missing Hit vs. Makeup Shot Under Virginia Count Rules

In the example below, we will use Virginia Count rules and minor power factor scoring. We will compare the overall hit factors between Example 1 where the competitor shoots one alpha and one mike vs. Example 2 where the competitor shoots one alpha, one mike, and one alpha makeup shot.

Virginia Count

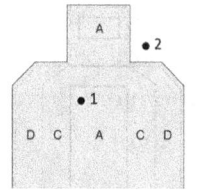 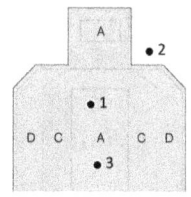

Example 1 – (2 Shots)	
(A) Alpha	5
Penalties	-10
Score	-5
Time (seconds)	1.25
Hit Factor	**0***

* Hit Factor cannot be negative

Example 2 – (3 Shots)	
(A) Alpha	10
Penalties	-10
Score	0
Time (seconds)	2.0
Hit Factor	**0**

Example 1: There are two shots taken at the target, but only one hit counts for a score, and the penalty miss is assessed for (-10) points. The miss creates a deficit of (-5) points because two scoring hits per target are specified in the written stage brief.

Example 2: There are three shots taken at the target, but only two hits count for a score. The extra makeup shot gets the higher points, but there were three shots taken, so the additional shot incurs a (-10) point penalty. (5+5) -10 / 2.0 = HF 0.

Note: Had the second shot hit the target in Example 2 for three total hits, there would be an additional (-10) point penalty for an extra hit, (-10) for the extra shot, and (-10) for the extra hit = (-20) penalty points.

FIXED TIME

Fixed Time stage rules place limits on time, the number of shots, and the number of hits per target. The Fixed Time stage format specifies the use of cardboard targets or disappearing targets where possible. Any extra time, shots, or hits will incur penalties. Extra shots are penalized from the shooting location, and extra hits are penalized at the target. You will see the Fixed Time format used in classifiers, standards, and short courses. Fixed Time rules do not use hit factor scoring; therefore, your actual scored points minus penalties is your stage score.

Fixed Time competitions are all about who can get the most points in the specified number of rounds within the set par time. The written stage brief will cover the specific time, zone scoring values, and number of shots you are allowed on the stage.

Example - Fixed Time Rules

In the example below, we will use Fixed Time rules and all competitors will receive points using minor power factor scoring zones. The written stage brief specifies three targets with two shots each, for a total of six rounds. The stage par time is five seconds.

Example: Seven shots were completed under the set par time of

five seconds. The best two hits count for score. T1 gets two alphas, T2 gets one alpha and one charlie, T3 gets two delta, and one alpha makeup shot. There is one extra shot on T3.

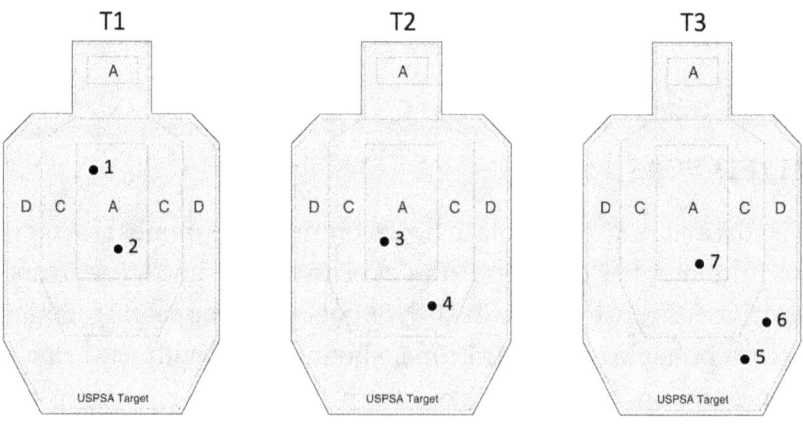

Fixed Time Example

Even though the makeup shot on T3 was an alpha, the extra shot and extra hit carry a (-10) point penalty each.

Target	H	A	C	D		M	P	NS
T1	2	2						
T2	2	1	1					
T3	2	1		2			2	
TOTAL	6	4	1	1		0	2	0
Minor Scoring	X5	X5	X3	X1		-10 Each	-10 Each	-10 Each
STATS	30	20	3	1		0	-20	0

Points Available	30
Hits	7
Best Scored Hits	24
Penalties	-20
Best Scored Hits – Penalties = Total Score	4
Par Time (seconds)	5.0
Fixed Time Score	**4**

CHAPTER 56
STAGE SCORING EXAMPLES

It is essential to understand the terms and math behind scoring a stage. All the previous scoring topics come together when you evaluate stage scoring. The following are the terms and definitions used in the full stage examples that follow:

- Points Available: the total number of points available on a stage for a perfect score. You can calculate points available by looking at the maximum value for each target.
- Stage Hits: the total number of hits on a stage that will count toward the competitor's score.
- Scored Hits: the number of points awarded across all the targets on the stage. For example, three shots are fired on a target, but only the best two hits will count toward the scoring total.
- Penalties: the total value of all penalties awarded on a stage.
- Total Score: the result of scored hits minus penalties.
- Time: how long it took to complete the stage in seconds.
- Hit Factor: the result of dividing total score by time.

Example Stage

The following stage is used to illustrate three scoring examples. The stage is a simple eight-round Comstock short course, with two shooting locations, three cardboard targets (T1, T2, T3), and two steel poppers (S1, S2). The T2 target has an accompanying no-shoot, and the T3 target has two black hard-cover areas on each side. All three examples will be calculated using major power factor scoring.

Competitors will start in Location 1 and shoot T1-T2, then move to Location 2 and shoot T3 and the two steel poppers.

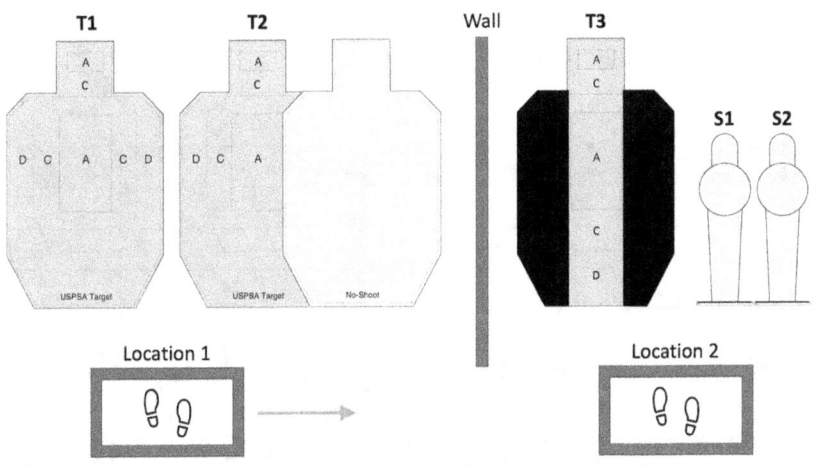

Stage Scoring Example

These next three scoring examples illustrate how speed and accuracy work together to calculate your stage performance through a hit factor score.

Stage Scoring Examples

- **Example (1) Hit Factor 8.0**: The competitor had a perfect run of 40 points in 5.0 seconds.

- **Example (2) Hit Factor 2.20**: The competitor had the same time as in Example 1 but had lower scoring hits and picked up two penalties.
- **Example (3) Hit Factor 5.0**: The competitor took more time, had better follow-up shots, and took a quick makeup shot to help offset the no-shoot penalty.

Stage Scoring - Example 1 Hit Factor 8.0

This example illustrates a perfect run of 40 points in 5.0 seconds.

The competitor completes the stage in 5.0 seconds. T1 gets two alphas, and T2 gets two alphas. Competitor successfully moves to the second shooting position, where T3 gets two alphas and both steel poppers fall.

Target	H	A	C	D		M	P	NS
T1	2	2						
T2	2	2						
T3	2	2						
Steel	2	2						
TOTAL	8	8	0	0		0	0	0
Major Scoring	X5	X5	X4	X2		-10 Each	-10 Each	-10 Each
STATS	40	40	0	0		0	0	0

Points Available	40
Hits	8
Best Scored Hits	40
Penalties	- 0
Best Scored Hits – Penalties = **Total Score**	40
Time (seconds)	5.0
Total Score / Time = Hit Factor	**8.0**

Adding it all up using major power factor scoring, we get:

T1 (5+5) + T2 (5+5) + T3 (5+5) + steel (2x5) minus 0 penalties = total score of 40 points. Hit factor is calculated by taking the total score and dividing it by the time taken to shoot the stage. E.g., 40 points / 5.0 seconds equals a power factor of 8.0.

Stage Scoring - Example 2 Hit Factor 2.20

This example illustrates a fast run of 5.0 seconds with lower scoring hits and a couple of penalties.

The competitor completes the stage in 5.0 seconds. T1 gets one alpha and one charlie. T2 gets one alpha and one no-shoot; and because there is only one scoring hit on T2, they also get a miss.

Competitor successfully moves to the second shooting position where T3 gets one alpha, one delta, and both steel poppers fall.

Target	H	A	C	D	M	P	NS
T1	2	1	1				
T2	2	1			1		1
T3	2	1		1			
Steel	2	2					
TOTAL	8	5	1	1	1	0	1
Major Scoring	X5	X5	X4	X2	-10 Each	-10 Each	-10 Each
STATS	40	25	4	2	-10	0	-10

Points Available	40
Hits	7
Best Scored Hits	31
Penalties	-20
Best Scored Hits – Penalties = **Total Score**	11
Time (seconds)	5.0
Total Score / Time = **Hit Factor**	**2.20**

Adding it all up, using major power factor scoring, we get T1 (5+4) + T2 (5+0) + T3 (5+2) + steel (2x5). Penalties are, T2 (-10 no-shoot) and T2 (-10 miss). Total scored hits = 31, less total penalties of -20 equals a total score of 11.

Hit factor is calculated by taking the total score and dividing it by the time taken to shoot the stage. E.g., 11 Points / 5.0 seconds equals a hit factor of 2.20.

Stage Scoring - Example 3 Hit Factor 5.0

This example illustrates a slower run than the first two examples, good scoring hits, and a makeup shot to offset a penalty.

The competitor is shooting major power factor and completes the stage in 6.0 seconds. T1 gets two alphas. T2 gets one alpha and one no-shoot. The competitor takes a makeup shot and gets a second alpha on T2. The competitor successfully moves to the second shooting position where T3 gets one alpha, and the second shot goes into the hard cover. The competitor takes a makeup shot on T3, receives a second alpha, and both steel targets go down.

Target	H	A	C	D	M	P	NS
T1	2	2					
T2	2	2					1
T3	2	2					
Steel	2	2					
TOTAL	8	8	0	0	0	0	1
Major Scoring	X5	X5	X4	X2	-10 Each	-10 Each	-10 Each
STATS	40	40	0	0	0	0	-10

Points Available	40
Hits	8
Best Scored Hits	40
Penalties	-10
Best Scored Hits – Penalties = **Total Score**	30
Time (seconds)	6.0
Total Score / Time = Hit Factor	**5.0**

Adding it all up, using major power factor scoring, we get T1 (5+5) + T2 (5+5) + T3 (5+5) + steel (2x5). Penalties are one no-shoot hit on T2 for (-10). Total scored hits is 40, less the total penalties (-10), which equals an overall score of 30.

Hit factor is calculated by taking the total score and dividing it by the time taken to shoot the stage. 30 points / 6.0 seconds equals a hit factor of 5.0.

SUMMARY

Shooting at your skill level and seeing what you need to see in order to get good scoring hits without penalties is the best way to ensure a higher stage score. Penalties are costly, as they quickly erase points. Makeup shots can offset penalties but will cost you in time.

CHAPTER 57
MATCH SCORING

Match scoring starts at the stage level and compares individual hit factors with other competitors to award a percentage of stage points. Individual stage points are totaled to determine the overall match winner.

In this example, we will use three competitors competing in a three-stage match. The first stage is a short course worth 60 points, the second stage is a medium course worth 100 points, and the third stage is a long course worth 160 points.

Competitors shoot each stage for scoring hits, penalties, and time. They receive a hit factor score per stage. The hit factor winner of each stage gets 100% of the available stage points. All other competitors will receive a percentage of the total stage points depending on how their hit factor compares to the stage winner.

Stage 1 – Short Course / 60 Points Possible

	Hits	Penalties	Total Score	Time	HF	%	Stage Points
Player 1	60	0	60	10.00	6.0000	100%	60
Player 2	60	10	50	10.00	5.0000	83%	50
Player 3	55	10	45	12.00	3.7500	63%	37.5

Stage 2 – Medium Course / 100 Points Possible

	Hits	Penalties	Total Score	Time	HF	%	Stage Points
Player 1	90	10	80	20.00	4.0000	100%	100
Player 2	85	10	75	25.00	3.0000	75%	75
Player 3	95	25	70	28.00	2.5000	63%	62.5

Stage 3 – Long Course / 160 Points Possible

	Hits	Penalties	Total Score	Time	HF	%	Stage Points
Player 1	140	0	140	28.00	5.0000	100%	160
Player 2	150	10	140	35.00	4.0000	80%	128
Player 3	130	10	120	32.00	3.7500	75%	120

Three Stage Match Scoring Example

When all stages are complete, the total awarded stage points for each competitor are added up to get their overall match points.

Match Results	Total Stage Points
Player 1	320
Player 2	253
Player 3	220

The match winner attains the highest total match points. *Note: Higher hit factors on large stages, with more stage points, can be more valuable to your overall match score.*

CHAPTER 58
MAKEUP SHOTS

OVERVIEW

In competition, you are on the clock to get as many high-scoring hits as you can in the shortest amount of time. It is better to take the time needed to see a good initial shot on target than having to do a makeup shot. From time to time, you will pull or miss shots if you focus on something else besides the current target.

Makeup shots are all about trading an improved target score for a longer stage time. Knowing when to take makeup shots is important to maximize your score. As your skills improve, you will start to see shots on target as you take them. When you know where each shot goes, it allows you to make better decisions that will improve your score. Knowing what to look for will help you make decisions quicker.

When You Should

Take makeup shots under Comstock rules *if* you can quickly complete a scoring hit that will offset a penalty.

Shots that miss the intended target and go into hard cover, no-shoots, or the berms are the best examples of when to take a makeup shot. If you hit a no-shoot, take your time and see what you need to see on the makeup shot. You don't want to hit it again and add to your penalties.

When You Should Not

You should not take extra shots when under Virginia Count or Fixed Time rules, because the penalty for taking the extra shot is greater than any scoring benefit.

For example, under Virginia Count and Fixed Time, you will receive a penalty of (-10) for extra shots and (-10) for extra hits. These penalties add up quickly and will erase your positive score. You are better off on these types of stages to get the scoring hits you need with each shot.

Anomalies - When it Depends

Makeup shots are all about trading an improved target score for a longer stage time, so doing a little math will inform your decision on how much time you are willing to trade to improve your target score. The next few examples are provided to help you get started modeling your own solutions.

The examples below all start with a benchmark example stage of three cardboard targets, two steel poppers, and two shooting locations. The stage example follows Comstock rules, with unlimited time, and stops on the last shot. The round count is unlimited. Scoring is assessed using minor power factor, and the best two hits on the cardboard will score.

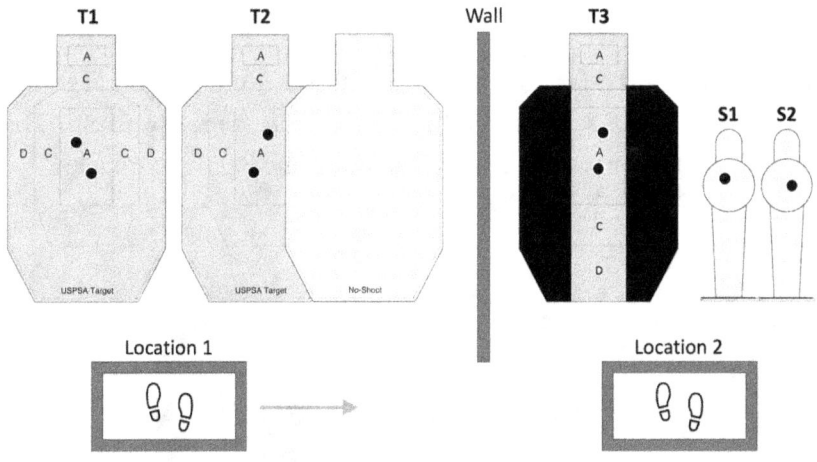

Benchmark Stage

In the benchmark example above, a competitor shoots T1-T3 getting all A (alphas) and both steel poppers fall. No penalties are assessed, and the total stage time is 5.0 seconds (the benchmark we will use as a perfect score).

T1(5+5) + T2(5+5) + T3(5+5) - penalties (0) / time 5.0 seconds = Hit Factor 8.0.

Points Available	40
Hits	8
Scored Hits	40
Penalties	0
Scored Hits – Penalties = **Total Score**	40
Time (sec)	5.0
Total Score / Time = **Hit Factor**	8.0

Next, let's look at how much time can be traded for a higher stage score where we do not shoot a perfect stage and consider whether we should take that makeup shot.

EXAMPLE: TAKING A MAKEUP SHOT ON ALPHA CHARLIE

The competitor shoots an alpha charlie (A + C) on T1 and achieves perfect score over the rest of the stage example. The overall hit factor would be 7.6 instead of the 8.0 benchmark.

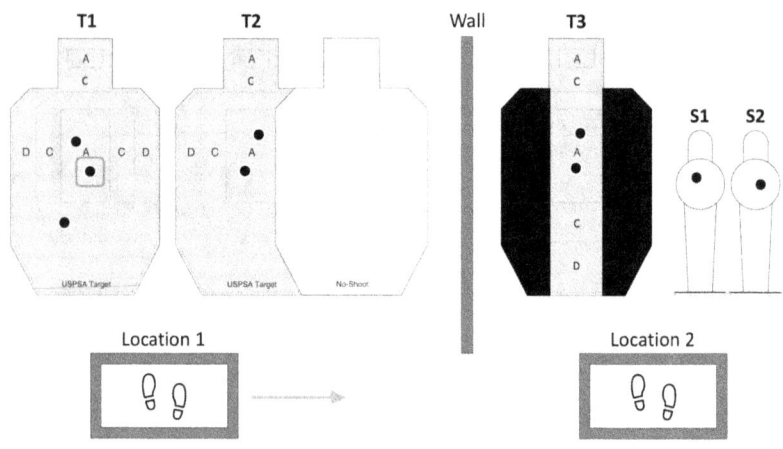

Makeup Shot - Alpha Charlie

Consider how much time can be traded to improve the score on T1.

	Benchmark Score	T1 A (alpha) C (charlie)	Make Up Shot on T1 Time vs. Hit Factor				
Penalties	0	0	0	0	0	0	0
Scored Hits – Penalties = Total Score	40	38	40	40	40	40	40
Time (sec)	5.0	5.0	5.1	5.2	5.3	5.4	5.5
Total Score / Time = Hit Factor	8.0	7.6	7.8431	7.6923	7.5471	7.4074	7.2727
Make Up Shot - Additional Time:			+0.1 sec	+0.2 sec	+0.3 sec	+0.4 sec	+0.5 sec

The chart above shows that anything longer than two-tenths of a second will negatively impact the current hit factor of 7.6, and the best it could improve the score is 7.8431. As 0.2 seconds is not much time to take a makeup shot in the A zone, there is a significant risk of lowering your overall score.

So, what should you do? In this example, take the C (charlie) and move on. The risk of lowering your score is greater than the benefit of getting a better scoring A-zone hit in 0.2 seconds.

EXAMPLE: TAKING A MAKEUP SHOT ON ALPHA DELTA

The competitor shoots an alpha delta (A + D) on T1, and a perfect score on the rest of the stage example. The overall hit factor is 7.2 instead of the 8.0 benchmark.

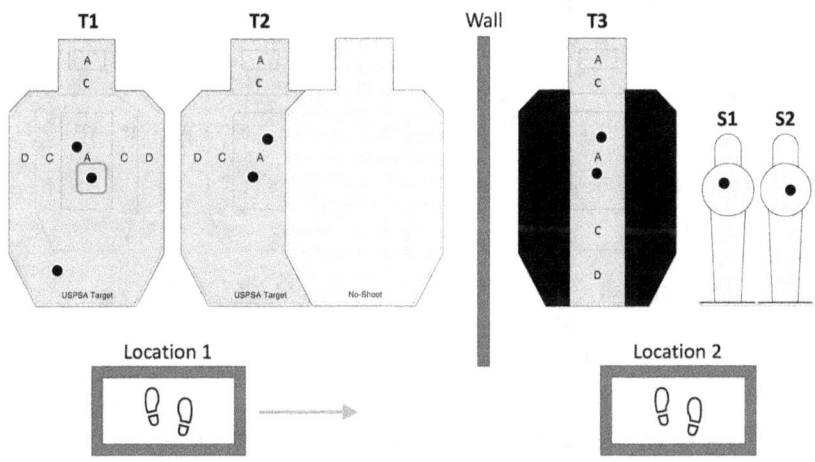

Makeup Shot - Alpha Delta

Consider how much time can be traded to improve the score on T1.

	Benchmark Score	T1 A (alpha) D (delta)	Make Up Shot on T1 Time vs. Hit Factor					
Penalties	0	0	0	0	0	0	0	0
Scored Hits − Penalties = Total Score	40	36	40	40	40	40	40	40
Time (sec)	5.0	5.0	5.1	5.2	5.3	5.4	5.5	5.6
Total Score / Time = Hit Factor	8.0	7.2	7.8431	7.6923	7.5471	7.4074	7.2727	7.1428
Make Up Shot - Additional Time:			+0.1 sec	+0.2 sec	+0.3 sec	+0.4 sec	+0.5 sec	+0.6 sec

The chart above shows that anything longer than half a second will negatively impact the current hit factor of 7.2, and the best it could improve the score would be 7.8431.

So, what should you do? In this example, it depends if you can take an A-zone makeup shot in less than half a second. The hard part is knowing that you pulled a D-zone hit and can take action quickly to correct it. If you need to transition back to see the target, you have probably exceeded the half-second window.

EXAMPLE: TAKING A HARD COVER MAKEUP SHOT

The competitor shoots one alpha and a hard-cover shot for one mike on T3, but the rest of the stage is a perfect score. The overall hit factor is 5.0 instead of the 8.0 benchmark.

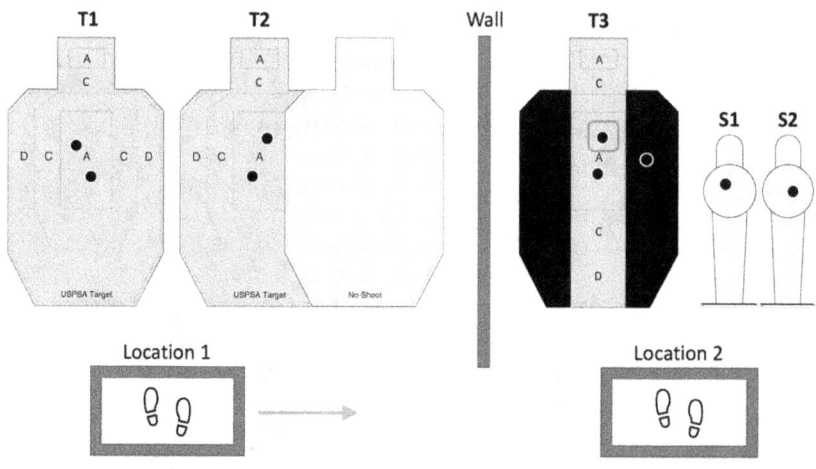

Makeup Shot - Hard Cover

Consider how much time can be traded to improve the score on T3.

	Benchmark Score	T3 Hard Cover Miss	Make Up Shot on T3 Time vs. Hit Factor				
Penalties	0	-10	0	0	0	0	0
Scored Hits – Penalties = Total Score	40	25	40	40	40	40	40
Time (sec)	5.0	5.0	5.5	6.0	7.0	8.0	9.0
Total Score / Time = Hit Factor	8.0	5.0	7.2727	6.6666	5.7142	5.0	4.4444
Make Up Shot - Additional Time			+0.5 sec	+1.0 sec	+2.0 sec	+3.0 sec	+4.0 sec

The chart above shows that anything longer than 3.0 seconds will negatively impact the current hit factor score of 5.0.

So, what should you do? In this case, if you don't see the second shot in the scoring zone, you have up to 3.0 seconds to get another alpha-zone hit. That is a large time window to get a second scoring hit. Therefore, if you were to take an additional second for an A-zone makeup shot, your hit factor would improve by 1.66 points.

EXAMPLE: TAKING A NO-SHOOT MAKEUP SHOT

The competitor shoots one alpha and one no-shoot on T2, but the rest of the stage is a perfect score. The overall hit factor is 3.0 instead of the 8.0 benchmark.

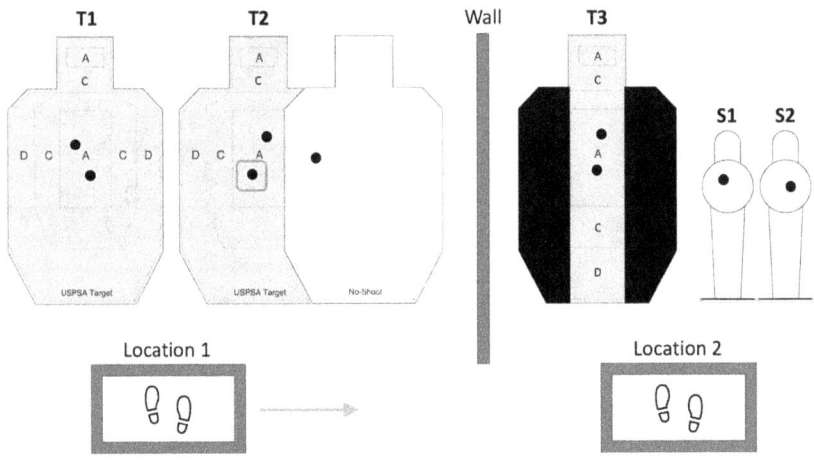

Makeup Shot - No-Shoot

Consider how much time can be traded to improve the score on T2.

	Benchmark Score	T2 No Shoot & Miss	Make Up Shot on T2 Time vs. Hit Factor						
Penalties	0	-20	-10	-10	-10	-10	-10	-10	-10
Scored Hits – Penalties = Total Score	40	15	30	30	30	30	30	30	30
Time (sec)	5.0	5.0	5.5	6.0	7.0	8.0	9.0	10.0	11.0
Total Score / Time = Hit Factor	8.0	3.0	5.4545	5.0	4.2857	3.75	3.3333	3.0	2.7272
Make Up Shot - Additional Time:			+0.5 sec	+1.0 sec	+2.0 sec	+3.0 sec	+4.0 sec	+5.0 sec	+6.0 sec

The chart above shows that anything less than 4.9 seconds will positively improve the current hit factor score of 3.0.

So, what should you do? Next time you see a no-shoot target, get a good sight picture, use proper technique, and try to achieve scoring hits rather than penalties. For every time you hit a no-shoot, you earn a ten-point penalty, and you will also be awarded a second ten-point penalty if you are missing a hit on the scoring target.

You can't erase the no-shoot penalty, but you can reduce the mike (or miss) penalty by taking a makeup shot. It is recommended that you get a good sight picture and achieve a good scoring hit, as you don't want a second no-shoot penalty. Therefore, if you were to take an additional second for an A-zone makeup shot, your hit factor would improve from 3.0 to 5.0.

SUMMARY

Makeup shots are all about trading stage time for an improved target score. It is better to have taken the time needed to see a good initial shot than having to do a makeup shot.

Comstock rules allow for makeups and can improve your score, especially when done to offset any missing hit penalties. Missing hits on scoring targets are excellent choices for makeup shots because you avoid missing your scoring points (+5), and you avoid the M (mike) penalty (-10) for a total of 15 points.

Non-scoring hard-cover or no-shoot hits are the best places to take a makeup shot, and when you see a no-shoot target, ensure you use a proper technique to achieve a scoring hit rather than a penalty.

Under Virginia Count and Fixed Time rules, the penalty for each extra shot is greater than any scoring benefit. Extra shots and extra hits receive a penalty of ten points each. Therefore, two penalties per shot can quickly add up to erase a positive score.

When shooting under these stage rules, you are better off taking the time needed to achieve a good score with each initial shot.

CHAPTER 59
CLASSIFICATION SYSTEM

Classification System

The USPSA classification system is a great way for competitors to see how their skills and performance compare with other members shooting in the same division.

Classifiers

When you compete at sanctioned USPSA matches, you will shoot stages called classifiers. Classifiers are specific courses of fire that are designed to measure a competitor's abilities within a division. They are a consistent way to evaluate accuracy, speed, and gun manipulations across different events. Classifier stages create consistency by following a measured layout and detailed stage instructions. You can view the most current classifier stage plans at https://uspsa.org.

Classification

Competitors shoot classifier stages to receive a hit factor score that is used to rank their performance within a division. Match officials upload classifier scores to the USPSA system where they are used to calculate members' classification levels. Each USPSA member receives an initial classification after they have competed in four different classifier stages within the same division.

After the initial classification, updated rankings are calculated from the best six of the most recent eight unique classifiers. If you compete in a major match and finish higher than your current classification, it can count toward improving your overall ranking for that division. Classification scoring uses the best competitor's division scores to calculate the performance levels of each classifier stage.

USPSA Classification Levels

- Grand Master = 95 to 100%
- Master = 85 to 94.9%
- A Class = 75 to 84.9%
- B Class = 60 to 74.9%
- C Class = 40 to 59.9%
- D Class = below 40%

Membership

You will need a USPSA member number to participate in the classification system, because member numbers are used to track scores and progress. You can sign up and get your member number at https://uspsa.org. Register this number at matches to start collecting your scores.

The USPSA classification system updates on a weekly cadence. The system takes into account your classifier and match results to determine your current classification level. It is important to note that clubs and events will need you to pay an activity fee before your data can be processed. Your match fees help cover administration and operating costs of the system.

Competing in local competitions is a lot of fun, but the USPSA classification system will help you track your division performance across multiple matches and seasons. As a result, many competitors focus on one division per season to improve their skills and classification level.

CHAPTER 60
TRAINING OUTLINE AND RESOURCES

Training Outline

In order to find the perfect balance of both speed and precision, a competitor has to build skill through practice. In any USPSA match, there are plenty of basic skills that are needed and required in order to get the best scores possible. To help you get started, below is a simple training outline of some necessary skills to review and practice in order to become more proficient with your firearm.

Basic Skills

Understanding and Practice of Safe Gun Handling - This one may seem obvious, but is so important it bears repeating. Anyone handling any kind of firearm should be familiar with safe gun handling practices and ensure they are followed at all times.

Grip and Trigger Control - Proper grip and trigger control are the first things to watch as you practice and look to improve your skills. You can practice your draw, building your grip, and prepping the trigger all in dry-fire. You will want to test these same skills at the range using live ammo to confirm your technique. Your grip can take some time to perfect, so investing time to get it right will pay off later.

Sights and Alignment - Practice seeing what is needed in your sight picture so you know where shots are going and can watch your sights lift and return on target. Watch your sights' alignment to the target so your focus is on only what is needed to make good scoring hits at different distances.

Check Your Accuracy - Confirm your accuracy. Adjust your equipment and technique as needed to ensure consistency. Keep notes in your journal of what you observe as you practice. USPSA is a balance of speed and accuracy, so knowing you can count on your technique to make good scoring hits will allow you to focus on other aspects of the game.

Accuracy at Speed - Combining accuracy with speed is the pinnacle of USPSA shooting competitions. Getting comfortable with speed is something all competitors need to practice so they can see things sooner, not just go faster.

Gun Manipulations - It's important to practice basic gun manipulations so you are not having to think about the mechanics of the movements as you are performing the operation. Shooting classifiers tests your ability to draw, load, reload, and get your gun up on target. Practicing these different gun manipulations in dry-fire will help to greatly increase your ability to perform in competition.

Follow-Up Shots - These are a good test of your ability to control recoil and execute a second shot on the same target effectively. It is important that you practice this at varying distances as you confirm your skills and precision. You want to see the sights return and settle quickly as you prep the trigger for the next shot.

Transitions - Shooting from the same location across multiple targets is a good way to practice seeing first and having the gun follow. You want to ensure your stance is supporting your movement and that you don't overswing as you transition. Knowing how to efficiently transition by focusing on a target and having the gun follow can significantly improve your overall stage times.

Measuring Your Time - Use a shot timer when you are ready to measure speed. Keep a journal of your par times for specific drills so you can see your progress. This way, you can see where it all adds up and find certain areas you can work on in order to improve.

Advanced Skills

In addition to the basic skills above, there are a few more advanced skills that can be practiced in order to take your game to the next level. While actually shooting can be considered a basic skill, learning to move correctly can be a larger contributor to your overall score. Learning when and where to move sooner can really help improve your times. Consider things such as:

Shooting on the Move - This will test your ability to see targets quickly, focus, and move smoothly. Using all of your acquired skills, try seeing and shooting your targets while on the move. Keep your eyes, gun, and sights as steady as possible as you track targets. You will need good upper-body form and smooth foot movement as you track and shoot targets. Good technique and trigger control will help you break each shot quickly so you can move on to the next target.

Practice Movement Drills - Another good way to improve is by practicing different movement drills. Practice moving left to right, back to front, and front to back, using safe gun handling the entire time. When you move from one shooting position to another, do it as efficiently as possible. Remember to confirm your last shot before you leave, and keep the gun up upon entry to the next position.

Dry-Fire - While not necessarily a movement drill, dry-firing is a great way to practice with your movement, manipulations, and other skills. Focus on one or two things to improve upon at a time.

They say that practice makes perfect, but really practice makes *permanent,* so take the time to practice things right. Learning the fundamentals and basic skill sets will set you up for long-term success, and the more you practice, the more improvement you will see. There is no greater feeling than demonstrating to yourself what you can do under the pressure of competition.

Resources

For additional material on USPSA Training Resources, see the companion website at https://pistolshootingsports.com/book-bonus.

PART VIII
YOUR FIRST MATCH

CHAPTER 61
GENERAL TIPS

At your first competition, let people know you are new. They will be happy to help you. When competing, speak up and ask the range officer for help if you don't understand something. Bring a positive attitude and demonstrate you are there to listen and learn.

Be Safe

When you are starting the sport, you want to ensure you are demonstrating safe firearm handling skills that will keep you and everyone else safe. Focus on simple execution of the basics and shoot for accuracy. Your knowledge of USPSA rules and competition principles will only grow as you observe and play.

Basic Skills

Practice your primary skills of gun handling in dry-fire so that your subconscious remembers what to do, and you don't need to rely on your conscious mind to control each skill. Your manipulations will only improve as you practice the basics.

· · ·

Jump in and Help

Everyone needs to help out when it comes to running a match. The people running the competition are volunteers and will appreciate your help to set up, run the matches, and put things away at its conclusion.

Range Officers

Respect the range officer. Range officers are experienced in running timers, scoring, and keeping your squad safe by watching for safety violations. At club matches, they can assist new competitors while they are on a stage. Listen to the advice they offer, ask good questions, and remember that this is a volunteer sport.

Stick With Your Squad

Competitors in USPSA are placed into a squad when they start a match. It's important that you stay with your squad and support them by helping reset stages and tape targets. Many of the people on your squad will be glad to answer questions or help you when it is not their turn to shoot a stage. Understand where you are in the order of competitors so you are ready to help or compete.

CHAPTER 62
MATCH OFFICIALS AND ROLES

MATCH OFFICIALS

Major matches allow many people to compete at a higher level of competition, but organizing these larger events requires several dedicated roles to keep things organized and moving. Below are some of the roles you will see at a major match.

- Match Director (MD)
- Range Master (RM)
- Chief Range Officer (CRO)
- Range Officer (RO)
- Chrono Officer (CO)
- Stats Officer (SO)
- Quartermaster (QM)

The Match Director (MD) is in charge of match administration and logistics to ensure a smooth-running event. This includes the coordination of support staff, range setup, scheduling, and squadding. They work closely with the range master and have authority over all matters except the rules.

The Range Master (RM) is the overall authority over all competitors and persons attending an event. They are responsible for all activities at the range before, during, and after a competition, and oversee overall range safety. They also operate the course of fire to ensure it adheres to USPSA rules—this includes making the final call on disqualifications. The RM works directly with, and reports to, the match director.

The Chief Range Officer (CRO) oversees all ROs and their activities. The CRO is looking for the correct, consistent, and fair application of all rules and stage briefs.

The Range Officer (RO) is the person who oversees compliance with USPSA rules and written stage briefings. ROs operate under the authority of a chief range officer or range master. The RO works at a stage level to issue range commands to participants and facilitate equal and fair competition. They ensure the stage is orderly and safe at all times. ROs will record times, score hits on targets, and determine any penalties that are attributed. The RO will also verify that each competitor's scoring sheet has been recorded.

The Chrono Officer (CO) reports to the range master and is the person who oversees the chronograph station. They are also in charge of the application of consistent rules for ammunition and equipment testing. In major matches, each competitor's ammunition is tested to ensure it meets major or minor power factor.

The Stats Officer (SO) operates under the range master to collect and verify scoring and compilation. They also publish final match results.

The Quartermaster (QM) is in charge of the range equipment used in the match (i.e., the targets, tape, paint, barrels, barriers, timers, batteries, staple guns, and scoring tablets). They report to the range master.

CHAPTER 63
WHAT TO BRING

When you attend your first USPSA or SCSA competition, bring a willingness to listen and learn as much as you can. Identify yourself as a new competitor so others can help you. People who compete in shooting sports are very welcoming and have all been in your position at some point. If you know an existing competitor that will guide you throughout a match, you will learn more about the sport faster.

Use existing equipment you or your friends already own. It is wise to hold off spending a lot of money when you begin learning the sport. As you practice and compete more, you will gain a better idea of where to invest your dollars. Get hands-on instruction around the use of your particular firearm and understand how its safety features work.

Review the chapter on "Shooting Gear" and ensure you have good ear and eye protection. Review the "On The Range" chapter so you understand and can follow all safety rules. Remember that all USPSA and SCSA competitions are held on cold ranges.

Test all the equipment you will be using before you get to a match. Get comfortable with how everything works so you will be able to focus on learning more details during the match.

Before attending a match, it is important to read and understand the rules of the game you will be playing. Refer to their respective websites for the most current version of the rules.

- Steel Challenge: https://scsa.org/rules.
- USPSA: https://uspsa.org/rules.

CHAPTER 64
WHAT TO DO

Shooting clubs want you to be successful and enjoy the sport. Therefore, don't be afraid to ask questions. Attend competitions with the mindset and equipment needed to be safe, compete successfully, and help keep the match moving so delays are not introduced.

Checklist:

1. **Equipment** - Review the chapter on shooting gear. Make sure you have appropriate safety equipment. Understand how to operate your firearm by consulting your manufacturer's documentation. Be proficient in the safe use and operation of your firearm. Know how to safety-check and demonstrate your gun is unloaded, safe, and empty of all ammunition.
2. **Ammunition and Magazines** - Bring the appropriate amount of ammunition and magazines for the match. For Steel Challenge, many people start with five magazines, so they have a fresh one available before

they start each string. For USPSA, take enough to get through a long course of thirty-two rounds with some left over for makeup shots. The right number of magazines will make your stage runs smoother and allow you to focus on how you're going to shoot a stage effectively.

3. **Divisions** - Review the different SCSA/USPSA divisions contained in this book to determine which one is best for you.
4. **Rules** - Review and be familiar with the official rules for your specific shooting sport. You can find the most current rules online. SCSA Rules: https://scsa.org/rules. USPSA Rules: https://uspsa.org/rules.
5. **Range Commands** - Review the section on range commands to become familiar with the terms. It is important to observe a competition first before competing.
6. **Safety** - Understand and follow all firearm safety rules. If you have questions, ask someone in charge. Each range will have safety rules that are specific to that venue. Refer to the section on range safety for more details.
7. **Stages** - Review the stages you will shoot at the match and understand how you will execute your stage plan before you step into the shooting area. Refer to the chapters on stages for your selected type of competition (i.e., stages for SCSA Steel Challenge, or course types and written stage briefings for USPSA).
8. **Arrive Early and Identify Yourself** - Come early to the match so you can help the club members set up. This will allow you to see firsthand how stages are put together. It will also be a way to meet new people in the process. Find someone who is in charge of the match and identify yourself as a new competitor. Each club will

want to review specific safety rules with you and cover how everything works. They may place you in a squad or pair you with someone who can help you during the match. At your first match, remember to be deliberately safe, ask questions, and take your time.

CHAPTER 65
IT'S YOUR TURN

Know where you are in the shooting order—when are you on deck, and when are you up. When it is your turn, arrive at the shooting area with enough loaded magazines and ammunition to complete your stage run. You will want to include enough rounds to do a few makeup shots.

Know who is running the stage. The range officer is the person running the timer and calling out range commands. Follow their direction and feel free to ask them questions when you are not sure.

Remember to keep your firearm pointed downrange at all times. Have a stage plan on how you will engage targets and the order you will shoot them. For Steel Challenge, be sure you know where the stop plate is. For USPSA, plan your movement, shot count, and reloads to maximize efficiency.

You have taken the time to educate yourself on the equipment, rules of the game, and how to be safe. When the range officer tells you to "make ready," it is time to have some fun!

PART IX
MEMBERSHIPS

CHAPTER 66
USPSA AND SCSA

Membership Benefits

You only need to become a member under either USPSA or SCSA, as the one membership will allow you to compete in both competitions. Your ID number can be used to access the USPSA phone app and members' area on the USPSA and SCSA websites. To become a member is easy—just register online to attain your membership ID at:

- USPSA site: https://uspsa.org
- SCSA site: https://scsa.org
- The websites are a wealth of information and can provide access to the following:
- Local clubs, which can be found by simply entering your address information to receive a list of active organizations near you.
- A list of local, state, sectional, regional, and national competitions.
- The latest rules in PDF format for you to download, print, and review.

- Classifier diagrams and written stage briefs with all the details on how to set up, shoot, and score.
- Classification systems to help you track your growth and performance. Simply enter your membership number.
- Links to online vendors where you can buy the latest gear and equipment, including official targets used in the competitions.
- Access to the National Range Officers Institute (NROI), which is where existing and aspiring range officers acquire the latest information on running and officiating matches.

Other Resources:

FrontSight Magazine - When you sign up for a membership, you have the option of receiving a *FrontSight* magazine. This magazine is a helpful resource for new competitors and includes articles about different area competitions, upcoming events, and useful ways to improve your performance. The subscription price is minimal, considering the benefits it provides.

USPSA App - This is a mobile app which is a great resource to stay connected with the latest information and online tools relating to USPSA events. The app is your key to online resources and acts as your membership card.

SCSA App - This is a mobile app designed to help members with classifier lookups, rules, finding clubs, and the latest information about the sport.

CHAPTER 67
CLUBS

Clubs facilitate and promote shooting sports. Becoming a member of your local club will connect you with the people who make this sport possible in your area. Clubs are usually a large membership body that supports and works with local ranges to facilitate and promote the shooting sports.

As mentioned above, you can find a local club in the area by searching on the USPSA and SCSA websites.

All clubs listed are affiliated with USPSA and SCSA, which means the club follows USPSA and SCSA rules for recognized matches and will post competitors' scores through the classification system.

Fees - Some clubs may charge a small fee to cover the costs of membership and/or the running of events. When you compete in matches, part of your entry fee goes toward the cost of targets, maintenance, leases, range dues, and uploading scores to the USPSA classification system.

CHAPTER 68
RESOURCES

Resources

Project Child Safe - Project Child Safe is one the largest safety education programs in the United States. It was started by the National Shooting Sports Foundation and is committed to promoting firearms safety. See their website for more information: https://projectchildsafe.org.

NRA Gun Safety Rules - The National Rifle Association was started in 1871 and promotes safe usage and firearm education through many programs in the United States. See their website for more information: https://gunsafetyrules.nra.org.

National Shooting Sports Foundation - NSSF was established in 1961 to promote, protect, and preserve hunting and shooting sports in the United States. The NSSF supports many safety and educational programs around firearms usage. See their website for more information: https://nssf.org/safety.

Lets Go Shooting - This site is a great resource created by the National Shooting Sports Foundations where new shooters can go and learn more about how to get started in the shooting sports. See their website for more information: https://letsgoshooting.org.

PractiScore - PractiScore is the most popular match management and scoring system used in competitive pistol shooting sports. It is designed to support several types of shooting competitions. The software runs on computers, tablets, and smartphones. By using PractiScore, scoring each competitor's accuracy and history is efficient and simplified. See their website for information and create an account: https://practiscore.com.

Steel Challenge Mobile App - Classifier lookup, rules, current ranking, and find clubs in your area. See their website for the latest information on features and downloads: https://scsa.org/app.

USPSA Mobile App - Classifier lookups, match results, find matches, rules, classifier diagrams, and locate clubs in your area. See their website for the latest information on features and downloads: https://uspsa.org/app.

GLOSSARY

Glossary

180 Rule: Refers to the 180-degree plane which follows competitors as they move on a stage.

A Zone: This is the highest scoring area used on USPSA cardboard targets.

Berm: A dirt mound that serves as a safety backstop.

C Zone: This is the second highest scoring area used on USPSA cardboard targets.

Caliber: Refers to the diameter of a firearm's bullet.

Cartridge: Assembled ammunition that includes a bullet, case, powder charge, and primer. It is also referred to as a round.

Centerfire: Firearms designed to shoot cartridges where the primer is located in the center of the cartridge's case head.

Chronograph: Instruments used to measure the velocity of ammunition fired from a gun.

Classifications: Defines a competitor's performance and skill level.

Cold Range: Refers to where all firearms must be kept unloaded until a competitor is operating under the direction of the range officer.

Course of Fire (COF): A design that defines the shooting challenge in terms of scoring method, targets, rounds, starts, and procedures. It is also referred to as a stage.

D Zone: This is the lowest scoring area used on USPSA cardboard targets.

Decibels (dB): A unit of measurement used to determine the intensity of sound or sound pressure levels.

Division: Defines the equipment and firearm used in a competition.

Dominant Eye: The eye your brain trusts to process sight information.

Dominant Hand: The strongest hand that supports your preferred trigger finger.

Dot Sights: Optical sight that uses a laser to project a sighting point onto a glass window or reticle. These sighting systems allow for fast target acquisition.

Double-Action (DA): A trigger type that performs two actions for each trigger pull.

Downrange: The 180 degrees of safe shooting direction toward the targets.

Dry-Fire: The practice of manipulating a firearm without any live ammunition. This is used in training to improve gun handling skills.

Grain: Used to measure the weight of bullets and size of a powder charge in a cartridge.

Hang Fire: When a round has a delayed discharge.

Hard-Cover Targets: Targets that do not incur penalties or points when you shoot them.

IDPA: The International Defense Pistol Association. They focus on sport-based defensive pistol techniques and simulated self-defense scenarios.

IPSC: The International Practical Shooting Confederation. They offer world-class competitive pistol shooting competitions that take place every third year and are hosted by participating countries.

ISSF: The International Shooting Sports Federation. They focus on Olympic-style shooting using air rifles and pistols, and shotguns for trap and skeet.

Live-Fire: Refers to shooting a firearm with live ammunition.

Minutes of Angle (MOA): A unit of measure used to align POA with POI. One MOA represents 1.047 inches at 100 yards.

Muzzle: The barrel of the gun where the bullet exits.

No-Shoot (NS) Targets: Targets that incur penalties when you shoot them.

Point of Aim (POA): Where the sighting system appears on the target as you aim the firearm.

Point of Impact (POI): Where the bullet impacts the target using a consistent aiming point.

Practical Shooting: Shooting sports that focus on point scoring using the balance between accuracy and speed.

Rimfire: Firearms designed to shoot cartridges where the primer is located in the rim of the cartridge case head.

SCSA: The Steel Challenge Shooting Association. They offer an annual Steel Challenge event, a steel target, speed shooting competition that appeals to a broad audience of shooting competitors.

Shooting Index: The ability to draw or transition to a target where the sights are visibly aligned and in the correct position in order to execute a shot.

Sight Picture: What you need to see on a target to execute an accurate shot.

Single-Action (SA): A trigger type that performs one action for each trigger pull.

Soft-Cover Barriers: Used to obscure scoring and penalty target areas.

Splits: The time recorded between shots on the same target.

Squib: A very serious condition where the bullet gets stuck in the barrel of the gun.

String: The number of shots and targets required to be executed on a stage.

Supportive Hand: The nondominant hand used to support your gun when using a two-handed grip.

Sweeping: When the muzzle of your firearm is aimed at yourself or a person as you move about a stage.

Transitions: The time recorded between shots on different targets.

Trigger Action: How a firearm operates with each trigger press. The trigger action releases the striker, or hammer, causing the primer on a cartridge to be struck and fire a shot.

Up-Range: The unsafe 180 degrees of shooting direction, away from the targets.

USPSA: The United States Practical Shooting Association. They offer competitive shooting competitions that focus on a competitor's ability to manage speed, power, and accuracy. Competitors compete for the highest scores and shortest times.

Walk-Through: A designated time to walk through and inspect the stage before you compete.

ACKNOWLEDGMENTS

Special Thanks:

The following people helped in the production of this book.

Scott Stirrat, Lucas and Eugene Dina, Fred Lindstrom, Seth Connors, Alex Kincaid

www.ingramcontent.com/pod-product-compliance
Lightning Source LLC
Chambersburg PA
CBHW071217080526
44587CB00013BA/1406